Alleged to have committed 21 known bank robberies on the Eastern Seaboard and convicted of only on one robbery in the small town of New Freedom. Pennsylvania Bill Hooker was sentenced by Judge Nealon at the federal courthouse in Harrisburg to serve 15-years. The judge sentenced Bill under Title 18 section 4205 ( B ) ( 2 ) allowing him to be released at the Parole Boards discretion. After serving 39 months, Bill was paroled to Cleveland. Ohio.

More than anything in the world. Bill wanted a new lease on life, and it came to happen in the most unusual way. He hoped that his lot in life would change with an indoor 8-men Jacuzzi named. Octapool. The logo would be an Octopus climbing out of a champagne glass. Because Octapool became a permanent fixture in the home. Unlike any other spa on the market, it qualified for Home Improvement Loans.

# Octopool:
# Some Kind of Crook II

# OCTOPOOL

## SOME KIND OF CROOK II

W.D BURNS

Mega House Publications

MEGA HOUSE PUBLICATIONS
P.O. Box 122
Brunswick, OH 44212
(440) 864-0494
www.megahousepubications.com

This book is an original publication of Mega House Publications.

Some Kind of Crook is based on a true story. The publisher does not have any control over and does not assume any responsibility for author or third party websites or their comment.

William Daniel Burns
SOME KIND OF CROOK II
Library of Congress Copyright 2011
TXu001815250
revised 2016

Editing, typesetting and cover design by J.D. Williams
(www.behance.net/jdwilliams)

ISBN:

Printed in The United States of America

10 9 8 7 6 5 4 3 2 1

# SOME KIND OF CROOK II

## INDEX

Dedication

To my wife, Bonnie Jean Burns. Thank the Lord for second chances. You complete my life!

Acknowledgments

Special thanks to Colleen Brown, for without her assistance this book would not have been possible. Props to my Editor in Chief and friend, Ronnie Jones.

# CHAPTER ONE
## THE VERDICT

Spruce Pine, North Carolina 1976. The bank robbery trial had lasted for three days. Bill's girlfriend Judy Osborn. was allowed to visit him at the holding cell while the jury was in deliberations.

"Ginge," she wept. "It doesn't look very good." Ginge was her pet name for Bill. The nickname came from the cartoon character Mr. Magoo who drove his car atop telephone pole lines. Mr. Magoo was sometimes called Gingus Con. and like Mr. Magoo, Bill had a history of wrecking automobiles. Judy shortened Gingus to 'Ginge'.

"It doesn't look all that bad." Bill replied, pondering the evidence given to the jury.

- Two men had robbed the bank. They wore nylon stockings over their heads distorting their faces. Two years has passed since the bank was robbed. Despite that, a bank teller identified Bill as one of the robbers. In hindsight, Bill wished he had asked for a line-up. Bill's attorney. Robert Pitts, objected when the prosecution asked to enter photos of the bank robbers wearing the nylon stockings. "I am objecting because this is the first time the photos have been made known to me. I don't know that I'm objecting to the photos being introduced into evidence." After looking at the photos, he quickly withdrew his objection. The photos made the in-court identification virtually impossible.

- An associate, Frank Kalita. testified Bill had confided in him as to how the robbery was committed. Frank was Judy's brother in-law and he had been convicted for robbing two banks. One in New Port Richie, Florida. The other in Wilson. North Carolina. It was only after his convictions that he cooperated. His credibility was questionable.

- A salesman from a New Car Ford Dealership in Maryland testified Bill had paid cash when he purchased a new 1974 Ford customized van.

Three weeks earlier Bill's co-defendant. Cleveland "Red" Miller had been convicted in a separate trial. The prosecutor offered Bill a concurrent sentence to testify against Miller. Bill flatly refused. At trial, Bill was offered a concurrent sentence in exchange for a guilty plea. Again, Bill refused.

While waiting in the holding cell Judy gave Bill two 20 Milligram Valiums.

The jury was escorted into the courtroom.

"Have you reached a verdict the federal judge asked the Foreman?"

"We have." the Foreman replied.

"And how do you find the defendant as to count one?"

"Not guilty!"

There was a moment of silence, then the judge asked. "And how do you find the defendant as to count two?"

"We find the defendant not guilty."

The courtroom erupted in joy. The jury smiled, and the federal judge pounded his wooden gavel on his desk while shouting.

"Order! Order in the court!" The judge stood up, unbuttoned the top of his black robe, ran his fingers through his noticeably gray hair, and announced. "That's the worst verdict I've heard in my history on the bench…"

Bill was somewhat dazed, the Valium's had worked their magic.

When he realized the jury had returned not guilty verdicts, he grinned, turned to Robert Pitts and hugged him giving him a slap on his back. Judy was holding their infant son, and smiling. Bobby Jenkins was beaming with joy.

After the judge quieted the courtroom, he continued. "However, that is your verdict. The jury is dismissed, to return in the morning to begin another trial. If there are no other pending charges against the defendant he is free to go."

"Your honor, the defendant is on Writ from Pennsylvania. He is to be returned for sentencing on a bank robbery conviction," the prosecutor offered.

"The defendant is to be remanded to the custody of the U.S. Marshals," the judge ordered dismissing the jury.

Bill leaned to his attorney and whispered, "You reckon he would've found me guilty?"

Judy whispered, "You're one lucky son-of-a-bitch, Ginge!"

* * *

With the trial over, Bobby and Mary Jenkins, their son Billy, and Judy and Bill's infant son were on their way back to Maryland. It was a beautiful day as Bill was escorted from the courthouse to the local jail by two U.S. Marshal's. As they crossed an asphalt street one of the Marshal's looked at Bill, smiled, and asked. "Did you do it?"

"Can they ever try me for that again?" Bill asked.

"No!" the Marshal replied assuringly.

Bill thought for a second, grinned, and replied. "No, I didn't do it!"

Once inside the small jail Bill paced the floor. He had been convicted with less evidence for robbing the bank in New Freedom, Pennsylvania. The F.B.I. had searched a house at 581 Gunpowder Road in White Marsh. Maryland. The search warrant claimed the residence to be William Daniel Hooker's. But, it wasn't! The house was Bill and Joanna Smith's residence. The warrant was invalid on its face, but the judge ruled Bill lacked "standing" to challenge the search of someone else's house.

As Bill was being returned to the Asheville City Jail, he was sitting in the backseat of the Marshal's car between two young Indian prisoners.

"Look out!" the Marshal riding passenger in the front seat screamed. A Semi with a trailer rounding a corner was tumbling to its side into the oncoming lane. The Marshal driving the car jerked the steering to the right to avoid being crushed by the falling trailer. The car ran off the road, flipped several times, and came to rest with its roof leaning against a tree. The Marshals crawled out through a window. The prisoners wearing leg irons, waist chains and handcuffs, couldn't move about freely and the Marshals weren't too concerned with getting them out of the car. They were taken to a local hospital by ambulance, then released with minor injuries.

* * *

At sentencing, for his part in the bank robbery in Spruce Pine, North Carolina Red Miller's attorney called Special Agent H. Thomas Moore to the stand in the hopes of obtaining a more lenient sentence. Moore testified that Miller was responsible for Frank Kalita's arrest and conviction and other bank robbers as well. Bill was the only "other" convicted bank robber. Miller robbed the bank in New Freedom, Pennsylvania with Bill, then told the F.B.I. where Bill was living.

"What you are really saying is that Miller was playing one end against the other. Isn't that correct?" the prosecutor asked Special Agent H. Thomas Moore.

"It is." Moore replied candidly.

Prior to Bill's trial, Frank Kalita was beaten by other prisoners in the Asheville City Jail. The headlines read: GOVERNMENT WITNESS BEATEN IN CITY JAIL.

* * *

Bill was returned to the federal prison in Lewisburg, Pennsylvania and housed in segregation until sentencing. At sentencing, the judge sentenced him to serve 15 years.

"Your honor," Bill asked. "Can I be sentenced under the provisions of 4205 (a)(2)?"

"You are!" the judge replied, explaining 4205 (a)(2) is now 4205 (b)(2). This meant Bill could be released at the discretion of the parole. Otherwise, the sentencing guidelines mandate the prisoner serve one-third of his.her sentence before becoming eligible for parole.

Within a week, Bill was transferred to the federal prison in Atlanta, Georgia to begin serving his sentence. Huge gray blocks of stone surrounded the perimeter of the prison and sparkled in the sunlight. The walls were topped with gun towers. A long passage of steps led to the prison's entrance, and for the first time in his life, he felt the loneliness that only someone who had walked those steps before him could understand.

"Where's the red carpet? Didn't you call ahead and tell them that I was coming? I'll be real disappointed if I don't get a room with a view?"

The U.S. Marshal chuckled, and replied. "Oh, I think you will be well satisfied with the accommodations."

"I hope so." Bill said gingerly. "Because so far, I'm really not all that impressed."

Like every other prisoner before him, Bill walked the long corridor to the property room where be was issued clothes, bedding, and assigned to a housing unit. He was assigned to a bunk in B-block which was an eight-man cubicle on the second floor facing the prison's entrance. Through the long row of barred windows, he could see the parking lot.

Bill first met Jimmy Burke in segregation at Lewisburg. Everyone knew the movie Goodfellas was about his life and the heist at the airport in New York. When Bill arrived at Atlanta Jimmy was already there, along with Bernard Chili and Lil Sal. Little Sal was an older mobster who worked in the produce department in the basement. If you were a friend of a friend who was from the east coast you were accepted into the crew.

Bill was quickly given a job working as a cook. Frank Kalita was also sent to Atlanta. After Miller's conviction, Frank knew that Bill had nothing to do with his arrest or conviction.

When he testified at Bill's trial, Frank deliberately testified to things that Bill could later prove untrue. They had no axe to grind, but they went separate ways. Frank lived on the opposite side of the block and worked in the prison's factory. Working in the kitchen as a cook gave Bill opportunities to make some quick easy money. Twice a month the prison fed steaks. The steaks were counted as they were given to the cooks, then counted a second time when they were grilled and placed on metal cookie sheets to be served to the general population. Next to the grill was the deep fat fryer. Bill melted the grease, then covered it with a lid. As he cooked the steaks, he chuckled and said. "One for you - and one for me," as he slid a partially cooked steak under the lid of the deep fat fryer and the grease would thicken turning solid white. At the end of his shift, the guards searched high and low for the missing steaks but never found them. The next day, Bill heated up the fryer, removed the steaks, then rushed over to the bakery where he cooked the steaks on the bakers rack. It was a huge gas powered rotisserie used for baking bread, cookies, and cakes. Two times around the steaks were cooked and the grease melted off. Lil Sal furnished the garnishings - tomatoes, onions, peppers. The sandwiches were individually wrapped in white paper. Prisoners wearing waist belts were called runners. They carried the steak sandwiches out, sold them, and split the profit with Bill. One sandwich sold for two packs of cigarettes.

Shortly after his arrival, on the way to his cellblock Bill heard an old but familiar voice.

"What's up nigga?"

It was James Percy Hall "Steeps". They served time together at the Maryland House of Corrections "Jessup's Cut" in 1968. Steeps was short, black, and in pretty good shape for his age. His hair was noticeably grayer.

"The last time that I saw you was on a Wanted Poster in a Post Office in Dundalk, Maryland." Bill grinned.

Steep's grinned. "Yeah, well just wanted to say 'hi'. Things are a lot different here. I have-to stay on my side and you have-to stay on yours." After talking for a couple of minutes they parted company, never to see each other again.

It was a Thursday night, and none of the runners showed up for egg sandwiches. So Bill stuffed the arm of his coat with thirty egg sandwiches. He was stopped leaving the chow hall, searched, and escorted to the Captain's office.

"What did you intend to do with the sandwiches?" The Captain asked, leaning back in his chair.

"I was going to sell them," Bill said flatly.

"I was hoping that you were going to tell me that you were going to eat them." the Captain smiled. "I wanted to see that!"

Bill was written a Major Misconduct ticket for Theft, but the ticket was never heard because Bill was transferred.

\* \* \*

Bill and Frank were both told to pack-up, that they would be leaving in the morning. Lil Sal checked with a friend who worked in the front office. He was told that Bill was leaving on a Writ of Ad Testificandum which meant he was being summonzed as a witness in a court proceeding. Lil Sal further explained that a Writ of Ad Prosequendum means that you are being prosecuted. Two brothers, Pete and Billy Grimes were facing a bank robbery charge in Virginia, but there was no reason to summonz him as a witness.

When Frank returned from his factory job, Bill asked him point blank. "Did you give a statement against Pete and Billy?"

Frank hesitated before answering. He said that he had discussed them but he didn't consider that a statement or anything that could be used against them.

"Why am I being summozed?"

"I have no idea." Frank swore.

The next morning the U.S. Marshals picked them up and drove to Virginia. They were housed in the segregation unit at the Reformatory in Petersburg, Virginia. One of their associates, Gary "Jabo" Wandrum, was serving time at the Reformatory for bank robbery. Bill sent him word that he was there. Jabo could probably get in touch with Billy and find out what was going on.

When Frank was in Atlanta, he feared for his life, there were nine murders in ninety days. Frank had made a statement. In his statement he said that Bill and Billy Grimes had entered the bank at night. Billy had opened the refrigerator and a noise spooked them. thinking they may have triggered an alarm. The prosecutor summonzed Bill because of Frank's statement. The well dressed young prosecutor confronted Bill in the bullpen. He said that he was going to put Bill on the stand and if he lied, he would charge him with perjury.

"Oh. I'm not going to lie," Bill chuckled. "I'm going to tell the jury how you threatened and tried to coerce me into testifying against the Grimes brothers."

The prosecutor did not call Bill to testify. Frank testified, and both of the Grimes brothers were convicted.

Judy and her sister Linda were planning to visit Bill and Frank at the County Jail in Virginia. On the morning of the day of the visit, two U.S. Marshals arrived to pick them up.

Instead of being returned to Atlanta, they were both being transferred to a federal prison in Washington State, McNeil Island.

"I'm not going!" Bill said flatly.

"What are you going to do?" Frank wanted to know.

"Follow my lead."

When the U.S. Marshals arrived, Bill sat down on the floor and announced that he wasn't going.

"Me neither." Frank snapped, sitting down next to Bill.

"Oh. You're going!" The U.S. Marshal retorted. "I've got a Court order. So, one way or another, you're going. If you resist, I will charge you with resisting."

"Oh. I'm not going to resist." Bill chuckled. "I'm just not going to assist."

After shackling their prisoners, the biggest U.S. Marshal said. "We can do this the easy way or the hard way."

"I guess you're going to have-to carry me." Bill grinned. Frank nodded his head in agreement.

Frank was sitting to the left of Bill, the closest to the door. The taller of the two Marshals grabbed Frank by the collar of his shirt dragging him out of the jail, down the steps, and across the asphalt parking lot with his ass bouncing hard on the pavement. At the car, he picked Frank up and tossed him onto the backseat like a rag doll. Witnessing that, Bill quickly decided to reevaluate his decision. Bill stood up and walked to the car with Frank screaming, "I'll kill you - you motha fucker!"

Frank's face was beet red, and Bill's chuckling simply added fuel to the fire.

Security stopped the airplane short of the runway and rolled out steps. Frank went up the stairway kicking and screaming. Once seated, he began shouting to the passengers that he was a political prisoner. The Captain told the Marshals that if they couldn't keep him quiet, he would have to leave the airplane.

"We've already thought of that." The U.S. Marshal smiled reaching for a roll of duck tape. He covered Frank's mouth wrapping the tape around his head. Frank began to hum the song "I've been working on the railroad" as loud as he could. The passengers laughed heartily. Even the Marshals were amused by his antics. When the plane was airborne, the Marshals asked Frank if he was ready to give up? Eat, or don't eat. It didn't make a difference to them one way or another. Frank decided to eat, but he never spoke a word to Bill throughout the entire flight.

Frank and Bill were housed in the Snohomish County Jail overnight. The bright colored lines painted on the floor and walls reminded Bill of a zoo. Prisoners were instructed to follow the yellow, red, pink, or blue line depending upon where they were being sent. The guards were all in need of an attitude adjustment. Prisoners were expected to keep their mouths shut and do as they were told, period.

In the early hours of the morning, the Marshal's arrived to pick their prisoners up. Forty-five minutes later, they were standing at the water's edge surrounded by a dense rolling fog. In the distance, they heard the sound of the ferry's horn as it approached the dock. In the front of the ferry there was a row of benches, and prisoners were to remain seated throughout the trip. There was only one way on and off the Island, the ferry. Dawn broke as they neared the prison. In the distance, the prison set on higher ground. Bill thought it looked like Alcatraz. Once inside the prison, Bill and Frank were escorted directly to the Warden's office. The Warden had heard of the incident with the Marshal's and although he was somewhat amused, he wanted to let them both know that he wasn't going to tolerate any misconduct at his prison.

Walking down the main corridor, Bill looked upwards noticing broken windows with loud pigeons sitting on rails inside the prison with pigeon shit covering exposed bars. Nasty was too clean of a word to describe the conditions. From the prison yard, snow could be seen atop Mount Rainer. In the summer months, Bill took a job working as a porter in the Psych Unit at night. The patients were locked up at night. Bill had a desk, a typewriter, a color television, and a huge bathtub. It was the best job in the prison, he thought.

When Bill appeared before the Parole Board, his release was set for May 1979 which meant he would only serve 39 months on his 15-year sentence. Cleveland "Red" Miller was going to have-to serve a minimum of five years. Frank was going to have to serve more time than Bill. And both Miller and Kalita had cooperated.

Billy Grimes was serving his sentence in Ashland, Kentucky. Pete Grimes was serving his sentence in Atlanta.

Gary "Jabe" Wandrum was serving his sentence at the federal reformatory in Petersburg, Virginia. And Frank Kalita and Bill were serving their sentences at McNeil Island in Washington State.

On April 5, 1977, after working all night, Bill went to the basement to turn in his laundry. He had agreed to pay a prisoner "Cowboy" five dollars a month to wash his clothes separate from the general population – and to iron his pants and shirts.

"Cowboy wants to see you in the back," the prisoner working the desk said, tossing Bill's clothes into a bin.

Bill walked past tumbling dryers and huge spinning washers and found Cowboy at work on an iron presser.

"Did you want to see me?" Bill asked.

Cowboy turned to face Bill, then suckerpunched him. Within seconds, Bill was on the cement floor being struck in the face by Cowboy and kicked by the other two prisoners. A guard tapped on the window and the beating stopped.

"Get the fuck out of here!" Cowboy snapped.

Bill slowly picked himself up from the floor and on wobbly legs, stumbled to the door. Using his right hand to cover his face, he hurried to the stairway and within minutes was inside the sanctuary of his eight-men cell. He washed his face in the white porcelain sink, examining the damage to his bloodied face. It was bruised badly.

Frank lived in an eight-men cubicle at the far end of the tier. Bill went in with him. Frank quickly agreed to help but said his knives were hidden at his workplace and he wouldn't be able to get to them until the next day. Bill returned to his cell, laid on his bed, and fell asleep. He slept through lunch and dinner. When he awoke around 7 p.m. his cellies wanted to know what happened to him. Bill wouldn't talk about it. His head was spinning and throbbing as he sat upright putting both feet on the floor. His hands cupped and felt his swollen face. His ribs were sore to the touch. Painfully, Bill stood up and walked to the sink. Turning on the cold water he splashed his face and toweled it dry. Then he wet his hair and combed it.

There were six double bunks in the cell. Two against the bars with a sliding steel barred door, one against each side wall, and two across the back wall. Between the two double bunks on the back wall was a four foot square sided cube. Inside that was a sink, mirror, and toiler shared by the eight men. The walls, beds, bars – everything was painted army green.

Bill left the cellblock at 10:45 p.m. walking down one flight of stairs and through the main corridor, past the dining hall, captain's office, and through a long tunnel leading to the prison hospital. Bill worked the night shift in the psych ward. The following morning he left work returning to his cell. As he exited from the tunnel he was met by Cowboy and another prisoner. Without saying a word Cowboy motioned with a hand gesture for Bill to follow him back into the tunnel.

"That's not happening!" Bill said flatly staring into Cowboy's hardened eyes. He stood six two, tall and lean with light brown hair. Both men were dressed in prison issued beige state pants with their shirt tails hanging out. Cowboy just stared at Bill saying nothing.

"As far as I'm concerned, it's over." Bill added.

Cowboy nodded his head, turned and walked back towards the cellblocks. Bill walked alongside.

"I've just got to know one thing." Bill asked.

"What's that?" Cowboy spoke for the first time.

"What was it over?"

"You just came at me wrong, dude."

With that said, Cowboy and his friend went one way, Bill another.

Bill went to see Frank and told him what just happened.

"If you had left work two minutes later or they had been two minutes sooner you would have been trapped in the tunnel." Frank concluded.

"I'm sure that was their plan."

"What do you want to do?" Frank wanted to know.

"I said it was over."

"And you believe it is?" Frank questioned.

"I don't know. But I said it was!"

The next day one of Bill's cellmates who was friends with Cowboy told him to watch his back. On April 7th, 1977 Bill went to the prison's theater to watch the movie The Hindenburg. Before the movie started Bill spotted Cowboy standing by the left wall of the auditorium talking with four other prisoners. He made a gesture at handing something to the other men, then pointed at the far side of the room. As the movie started and the lights dimmed, Cowboy and the two prisoners seated themselves on the right side of the theater. The other two prisoners seated themselves on the left side, a couple of seats in on about the sixth row. Bill was seated about five seats in on about the fifteenth row. Tom Colvin was seated about five seats in on the thirteenth row.

About halfway through the movie "Pill line" was flashed on the right wall next to the movie screen.

As prisoners exited to go get their nightly meds a lighter flickered on the right side, then two prisoners started fighting. Not wanting to wait around and see if this escalated into a riot, as the guards ran to take control Bill left with the prisoners going to med line. Bill showed up for work early. Within minutes Tom Colvin was brought in on a stretcher. He had been stabbed twice, once in the chest, then in his neck. The knife was left lodged protruding into his brain. As Colvin laid quivering on a stretcher the phone rang. Whoever was on the other end of the phone told the guard to preserve the knife. The guard asked Bill for towels and he handed him two. The knife was pulled from Calvin's neck and placed inside a clear plastic bag. Colvin died en route to the hospital.

Within twenty-four hours Cowboy and the four prisoners were locked up in segregation. The flicker of the lighter was the signal to start the fake fight. While everyone was distracted one prisoner stood guard while the other stepped in behind Colvin and stabbed him twice.

Two days later during the evening meal Bill's table was surrounded by guards who had orders to escort him to the Captain's office.

"I've got orders to lock you up. There's a contract on you in population." The Captain announced.

Bill was placed in segregation on the same range as Cowboy and the four prisoners charged with Colvin's murder. The next day the Institutional Investigator called Bill out. He was aware of the assault in the laundry.

"Do you know where I'm housed? I'm on the same range as the guys charged with the murder. I've got nothing to say until I'm moved!"

Bill was moved from the prison to the maximum security floor at the Snohomish County Jail. He had no viable reason to be there.

Bill's first acquaintance was Danny Torres Macias.

February 1977's edition of Penthouse magazine featured Danny. "The New Mafia – mean, mobile and Mexican." He was documented distributing heroin in ten different cities. Danny told Bill that he sensed something wasn't right with his being there adding that he didn't care as long as it didn't affect him.

Two weeks later Bill was flown on a charter two engine turbo prop to San Diego and placed in the witness protection unit at the Metropolitan Correctional Center. It was there he met Jimmy "The Weasel" Fratiano. Jimmy was a hitman for the mob.

Bill filed a motion in federal court and John J. Cleary of the Federal Defenders Office was appointed. John's greatest case was he was part of the defense of Son of Sam.

The five guys charged for the murder of Thomas Colvin were acquitted.

A year later, Bill was transferred to Memphis, Tennessee. The Federal Correctional Institution was very nice. Carpeted floors, single rooms, a pool table in the Unit, and a room with a color TV.

Roy Clark gave a performance inside the prison. A Semi was parked in the grass and a stage extended out from the side of the Semi's trailer. Roy

Clark and a young boy played banjos and bluegrass music. After the show, Bill returned to his room and wrote a song.

Burnin Biscuits
I woke up early morning
With Honey on my mind
burnin biscuits on the stove
and some memories of old times.
Honey says she loves me
Yes, she loves her gamblin man
but lately I've been losin
just a little more than she can stand.
Last week I lost her wedding rings
in a game in Tennessee
then I lost our everything
and now Honey's leavin me.
I've played the field in Vegas
placed wagers at the track
spent every dime in misery
and swore that I'd be back.
I said, I woke up early morning
with Honey on my mind
burnin biscuits on the stove
and some memories of old times.
Honey says she loves me
she loves her gamblin man
but lately I've been losin
just a little more than she can stand.
Well, a winner never loses
and a loser never quits
but if you think that I'm a winner
on that I'll take side bets!

The F.B.I. circulated a flyer across the Eastern Seaboard crediting "The Hooker Gang" for 21 known bank robberies. The flyer listed the names of the bank, location, mode of operation, described the manner each bank was robbed, and the amount of money taken from each bank. Twice the F.B.I. had tried and failed to indict Bill for a bank robbery in Bristol, Tennessee. In that robbery $104,000 was taken. In one year, Bill purchased nine new cars, lost $31.000 at Ceasars Palace in a weekend, and lived a life of luxury. Tom Jones was the featured singer at Ceasars Palace and Evel Kneveil was on closed circuit TV at Ceasars when he attempted to jump Snake Canyon.

Within three months the contract followed Bill to Memphis. Bill was placed in Segregation. Again, Bill petitioned the court. He was given the option of returning to San Diego (but there was a waiting list) or going to the unit at the Metropolitan Correctional Center in Chicago now.

# CHAPTER TWO
# THE PLAN

Bill, along with Gerald Burns and Richard Biggerstaff made Plans to build a pool. Octopool would be the first Jacuzzi to become a permanent fixture in the home qualifying it for Home Improvement Loans. Their insignia was an Octopus climbing out of a champagne glass. Jerry paroled first, to Columbus, Ohio. Bill felt the game was over. his debt to Society paid. Instead of returning to Baltimore, he requested to be relocated. Richard Biggerstaff promised to secure the financing for Octopool upon his release. On May 31, 1979 Bill was released on parole and relocated to "Cleveland," Ohio.

Gerald "Jerry" Burns was no relation to Bill. They had met in prison, formed a friendship, shared common interest, and they called each other brothers. They had a Plan and together they hoped to get rich beyond their wildest dreams.

In 1979 Cleveland, Columbus, and Cincinnati were the three most prosperous cities in the United States according to the articles and information they had read. Their plan was to manufacture an eight-man jacuzzi thoughtfully named Octopool. None of the other home spas qualified for Home Improvement Loans. Because Octopool became a permanent fixture in the home, it qualified. The timing was perfect. The United States was experiencing a recession and people were spending more time at home. Octopool had great selling features. There was no out of pocket expense for the homeowner. Local builders who installed swimming pools were lacking sales during the winter months. Bill and Jerry's plan included selling franchises.

Ten months before Bill, Jerry was paroled and relocated to Dayton, Ohio along with his girlfriend, Lynn Bailey. She would have followed Jerry to the ends of the earth. Lynn had some money saved, a 1977 canary yellow Cadillac Coupe Deville, and at Jerry's urging she had moved from California renting a small apartment in Dayton, Ohio. She found employment as a legal secretary for a prominent attorney.

Lynn was petite with short blonde hair. Jerry was six feet, two hundred pounds, burly like a bear, and he sported a mustache and goatee.

Jerry and Bill quipped they could sell snow tires in Florida, or snow cones to the Eskimo's. Jerry's personality was as big as he was. They both knew the difference between a salesman and a closer. A salesman sells neck ties and shirts in department stores, while a closer sells a thought, an idea, with nothing more than words. And Bill and Jerry, they were closers. That, Bill was sure of!

After Jerry's release, he found a job selling swimming pool's for a local contractor.

As Bill's release date neared, the days were taking their toil and passing at a snail's pace.

The U.S. Marshalls rented Bill an efficiency apartment at the Buckeye motel on Lorain Avenue in North Olmstead, Ohio.

On May 31, 1979 the U.S. Marshals picked Bill up at the airport and took him to the Buckeye motel. It was only five minutes from the airport.

Bill checked in, got his room key, went to his room, sprawled across the bed and instantly felt the comfort of the cool thick mattress. He laid there for several minutes pondering his next move. As he surveyed the efficiency there was a small refrigerator, a hot plate, and an ice bucket. At the far end of the room, there was a pink counter top with a sink and a large rectangular mirror. To the left, there was a door leading to the bath, shower, and toilet. A color TV hung in a corner. Next to the bed was a nightstand, a lamp, a phone, and a remote for the TV. Inside the nightstand, he found a Bible.

Bill clicked on the television, grabbed his duffel bag and started unpacking what few treasured items he owned. A few clothes, hygiene products, and a blueprint of Octopool. After he showered, he laid back on the bed and relaxed, the phone rang bringing him back to reality.

"Hello?" Bill answered.

"Have a nice trip? Sorry that I couldn't pick you up at the airport, but in the real world we have to work regular jobs. Lynn and I will be there Friday night." Jerry promised. "Meanwhile, buy a map. Take a walk, and get acquainted with Cleveland."

"Yeah, right. I'm not giving much consideration to walking very far, brother."

Jerry laughed, assuring Bill, once again, that he and Lynn would be there Friday night before ending the call.

Hunger pains made Bill think about getting something to eat. He left the comfort of the motel room, turned right, and walked a half block discovering a small hole in the wall Irish Pub called The Lamp Light. Greenery grew wild against the red brick face of the building. Bill looked at his watch, thinking someday he would buy himself a nicer one. The cheap Timex kept accurate time, it was almost four o'clock. There were several booths inside the bar and a long counter with red covered barstools. There were three patrons, and a very friendly bartender who smiled, and asked. "What's your pleasure?"

"Seven and seven." Bill replied, seating himself at the counter. The smell of food cooking filled the air. Minutes later, Bill ordered a steak sandwich and French fries.

The bartender/owner extended his hand in friendship and introduced himself as Gary. He was six foot, thin, with brown hair and hazel eyes. Bill guessed Gary to be in his late thirties.

After two drinks and a tasty meal, Bill decided to go for a walk. Within walking distance he found a McDonalds restaurant, a Goodwill store, and a small shopping plaza. He ventured across the street entering the Goodwill store. Once inside, he saw racks of suits, jackets, and coats. Shirts and pants were sized, neatly folded, and displayed on tables. Bill purchased two suits that looked like brand new, four pair of Hagger slacks, several shirts, and the total amount spent came to less than twenty dollars. Returning to the motel room, Bill looked at his watch contemplating his next move. It was six o'clock. He sat down on the cool mattress, picked up the phone, and dialed the number to his friends' home in Maryland.

"Hello?" Mary answered. "Well, hello there, gorgeous."

"Oh, my God. Where are you? Are you out of prison?"

"I'm in a motel in Ohio."

"No, you're not. Are you really? Don't tease me, Bill."

Mary giggled, then shouted. "Bobby, it's Bill. He says that he's in a motel in Ohio."

"Hello?" Bobby chuckled, taking the phone from Mary.

"How are you doing?"

"Good. Are you really out?"

"Yes, I am. I'm residing at The Buckeye motel in North Olmstead, Ohio."

"What are you doing in Ohio? Do you know someone there?"

"I know a bartender named, Gary." Bill chuckled.

Bobby laughed, then asked. "When are you coming to see me, son?"

"I'm hoping to fly to Maryland next weekend. I need some transportation, can you help me out?" Bobby worked as a mechanic and he bought and sold vehicles to earn extra money.

"I don't have anything right now." On second thought, Bobby added. "Let me talk to Mary."

The bond between Bill and Bobby was unbreakable. Bobby often said that he trusted Bill more than he did his own kids, and he meant that with all of his heart.

After talking with Bobby, Bill tried on some newly purchased clothes. Surprisingly, they fit as though they were tailor made. Bill stood in front of the mirror admiring himself. The thought of his meeting a girl amused him. What would he say? "Hello, my name is Bill. I just got out of prison. I have no job, no car, but would you like to go back to my motel room with me?" He just didn't see that as a possibility, not even a remote one.

The phone rang, and he answered it.

"I just got off work, thought I'd call and check on you. Is everything okay?"

"No, I'm still searching for the naked girl and the bottle of champagne."

"There's an inflatable doll in the closet." Jerry snapped, without missing a beat. "And she doesn't drink, so you don't need the bottle of champagne," he chuckled.

Jerry had a surprise that couldn't wait until the weekend. He wanted to let it be known now. "I built a prototype of Octopool," he announced with pride. "It's not up to manufacture standards, but it looks and works good."

"I can hardly wait to see it!" Bill said excited by the thought.

"Well, you're going to have to wait. It's too big to be carted around." Jerry laughed. They had no funding for the project until Richard was released, he was paroling to his home state of Oklahoma in five months.

Bill was present for the last call at The Lamp Light. While inside, it had rained. The well lit street looked like a neon rainbow. The air was cool and refreshing. Not wanting to return to an empty motel room, Bill decided to go for a walk through the neighborhood. There were concrete sidewalks, well manicured yards, with tree branches that hung well over the sidewalk. On the return walk, less than a block from the motel, Bill spotted several potted plants sitting on top of a porch railing. One plant stood out from the others, it had huge green leafs that glistened in the dim light. Bill felt the plant needed rescuing. It was as if it was saying, "Take me with you!" At a brisk pace, Bill grabbed the plant and carried it to the motel room. Once inside, he named the plant "Ralph".

While most people have dogs, cats, hamsters, birds, or goldfish as pets. Bill had a rubber plant that he affectionately called, Ralph.

\* \* \*

As promised, Jerry and Lynn arrived at the Buckeye motel around eight o' clock Friday night. It was a two hour drive.

"It's good to see you." Jerry hugged Bill, giving him a slap on his back. Lynn smiled approvingly, and hugged Bill as well. Stepping inside the room, they talked for the better part of an hour. Bill told them about the Irish Pub, his shopping at the Goodwill store, and how he had acquired his plant, Ralph.

"Oh. That's nice," Lynn giggled. "I bet you would have felt pretty stupid had you got caught and been returned to prison for stealing a plant."

Jerry laughed heartily, but agreed. "You can't be doing dumb shit! I rented a room, so we've got the weekend to help with whatever needs to be done."

"My top priority is finding an apartment to rent." Bill said, looking around the tiny room.

Jerry and Lynn went to their room, freshened up, then called Bill. "Let's go to the Pub and get something to eat." Jerry felt that would be a good place to ask questions and get an idea of where to start looking for an apartment.

Gary recommended Parma Heights. He said that it was in a nice neighborhood and within walking distance to the Parma Mall, grocery stores, and banks. There was a favored watering hole called The Ground Round. And anything else that Bill may want would be within walking distance.

Before returning to the motel, Jerry filled the Coupe Deville with gas and purchased a local map. "Get some sleep," Jerry told Bill. "Because we're going to get an early start in the morning."

The next morning Bill awoke to an unfamiliar sound, the phone ringing. Jerry was on the other end. "Wake up! We will be picking you up in ten minutes."

Bill quickly showered, shaved, and dressed. Then he browsed through the Yellow Pages looking for apartments in Parma Heights. An ad caught his eye. It was a highrise building known as Regency Towers. It featured security, underground parking, elevators, recreation rooms, tennis courts, an indoor swimming pool - and much more. The amenities were plentiful! When Jerry arrived, Bill suggested they go there first. Lynn quickly suggested they have breakfast first.

"I meant after breakfast." Bill laughed.

Lynn smiled. Gary had told Bill where there was a Country Kitchen restaurant nearby, and he now found himself wishing he had paid more attention to the directions.

"You just ran a red light!" Lynn screamed, hitting Jerry's arm.

Jerry grinned, promising that he would stop twice for the next one. Lynn found the two of them impossible to deal with, and gave a disgusted sigh of defeat.

After a hearty breakfast, they drove directly to Regency Towers. It was a twenty minute drive. There was a hospital across from the Parma

Mall. Behind the hospital, there were four highrise buildings, a complex known as Regency Towers. Jerry parked in the front lot. As they entered the glass foyer, there was a panel listing the names of apartment residents. Next to each name there was a button to press that rang the apartment and the resident could view the person requesting entry on closed circuit TV. They could buzz the visitor in, talk over the intercom, or simply ignore the visitor. The lobby's carpet was a plush red, green, and black design. Several soft sofas and chairs welcomed waiting guest. Washers and dryers were on every floor.

Bill filled out an application, paid the first and last months rent in cash, and made plans to move in on the first of the month. The apartment he chose was on the first floor at the far end of the hallway. An exit door allowed for easy access to the rear parking lot, community clubhouse, tennis courts, and indoor pool. While the upper floors offered balconies with spectacular views, his preference was the easy entrance. The apartment had two bedrooms, one bath, living room, dining room, and kitchen. The master bedroom had a walk-in closet. It was furnished with a refrigerator and dishwasher, and the new carpet was emerald green.

Just outside the rear entrance were several shopping carts. Some of the tenants walked to the Kroger's Supermarket, which was only a block up the street on the left, then pushed their groceries home in the carts. Once or twice a week, the store manager would send an employee to retrieve the carts.

The trio drove around Parma Heights, checking out the area. They parked, and walked the Parma Mall from one end to the other. On the opposite side of the street was the Ground Round, a bowling alley, and Best Products. What they hadn't passed was a furniture store, and the apartment was unfurnished.

They stopped for lunch at the Ground Round. Lynn ordered a Coca-Cola while Bill and Jerry ordered Crown Royal on the rocks toasting their business venture, Octopool.

"Did you see the girls laying on towels on the concrete slab outside of the Community swimming pool?" Jerry asked Bill.

"What were you doing looking?" Lynn asked, rolling her eyes.

The waitress told Jerry there was a furniture rental store on Pearl Road, and she gave directions. This time, Jerry paid attention to the directions. It was less than a ten minute drive. Bill picked out a bedroom outfit, a living room set, end tables with lamps, a coffee table, and a dining room table with four chairs. Lynn co-signed, and Bill scheduled a time for delivery.

Bill's rent at Regency Towers was $780 a month and his furniture rental $160. The U.S. Marshalls Service allotted him $1500 a month living expenses.

Late Sunday afternoon, Jerry and Lynn said their goodbyes, promising to return to help Bill move.

The days passed slowly. Bill had never been so bored, or eaten so many bologna sandwiches and potato chips. At night, he looked forward to visiting the Irish Pub until closing.

Bill caught an early bird flight to Baltimore, arriving at ten in the morning. Bobby greeted him at the gate with a big grin, and a hard, but loving, slap on the back. "It's good to see you, son."

"How is everything? And everyone?"

"Good! But you will never guess who stopped by the station yesterday?"

Bobby quickly answered, "Lee Chambers! He asked if I had heard from you. I told him that you were out of prison, and that I was picking you up at the airport this morning. He gave me his phone number and told me to tell you to give him a call."

"I'm going straight!" Bill announced. Bobby grinned, doubting that.

"I mean it! I've got a new direction, and I intend to turn over a new leaf. Believe it or not, I have Plans to build an 8-men Jacuzzi named, Octopool. Our logo is an Octopus climbing out of a champagne glass."

"If you're serious, that's the best news I've ever heard. But I never thought that I'd live to see that day."

It was going to be nice to see Lee, Bill thought. They grew up breaking into houses, businesses, and cracking safes. On one job Bill got away, and Lee was caught inside the building. Lee never snitched, and that made their bond even stronger. Lee was a good egg!

Bobby left to return for work, he would be home at five o' clock.

Bill called Lee. The phone rang several times before being answered.

"What's up?" Bill chuckled. "When did you escape?"

"I didn't. They let me go for good behavior."

"I seriously doubt that." Lee snickered. "When did you get out, and where are you living?"

"I was released ten days ago. Right now I'm living in a motel in Ohio. But I just rented a two bedroom luxury apartment in the suburbs of Cleveland. I'll be moving next weekend. I don't have a phone yet, but I'll give you a call as soon as I get settled. I'm only here for tonight, and tomorrow. Sunday I will be leaving. How are things with you?"

"Not good. I'm two months behind in my rent. I'm so broke the cockroaches moved out! My wife, Jenny, left taking our two kids with her. They're living in Georgia with her mother. She said that she's going to divorce me, and I think she means it this time."

Bill heard the desperation in his friends voice. Lee's blue eyes and baby face was always a hit with the ladies. And his southern drawl was still imminent when he spoke. Bill teased Lee that his long hair was an inch short of his being a hippie.

"I've got a spare bedroom, if you need a place to lay your head."

"I just might take you up on that." Lee replied, in a serious tone.

"You are more than welcome, my friend. Anytime!"

"Are you on parole?"

"Yes, and no. I called my parole officer and all I'm required to do is mail in monthly reports."

"Can you write?" Lee chuckled.

"Yeah. I learned by writing bad checks."

"How do you like Cleveland?"

"So far, so good. I have met a friendly bartender, and the apartment where I'll be living has an indoor swimming pool freshly stocked with beautiful girls in string bikinis looking for studs to fulfill their wildest fantasies."

"Young studs? Well I guess that leaves you out." Lee chuckled, then asked. "Is there really an indoor pool?"

"And every other amenity that you can imagine. On a scale of one to ten, it's a solid nine."

"I've already started packing my bags. Are you sure that you don't mind?"

"I don't mind. But I have to tell you, I've gone straight. I have a plan in the works and it's one hundred percent legitimate."

"I'm good with that." Lee promised.

After saying their goodbyes, Bill felt good knowing that he wouldn't be living alone. Lee would be there for better, or worse. If things went sour, he could depend on Lee to have his back.

* * *

Dinner time. Mary had a checkered apron wrapped around her small waist and she was hurrying around the kitchen. To the refrigerator, opening cabinets, kitchen drawers, grabbing boxes and utensils. She mixed things in bowls, rushing from the counter to the stove. Yet, in all of the hustle and bustle, she was still well organized.

Bill seated himself at the breakfast nook. sipped a hot cup of coffee, while admiring Mary's beauty. She was much younger than Bobby and the two of them had weathered many stormy days. They made a great team. They were a family! Mary bore a strong resemblance to Loretta Lynn. Her long brown hair fell to her waist, and her mannerism matched Loretta's to a tee.

Bobby had just returned from work, he was in the bathroom washing up. Their son, little Billy, was downstairs in his bedroom playing drums. Their daughters, Karen and Sandy, were out and about, but everyone would be at home sitting at the dining room table soon - as if by ritual. Bill had been missing for quite awhile. But he was back, at least for now.

"Come here." Bobby smiled, looking squarely at Bill. "I've got something that I want you to see."

Bobby opened the door to the garage, walked inside, and Bill followed.

In one corner were brooms, rakes, snow shovels, and an assortment of garden tools. There was a long work bench with a grinder, mechanic tools, and a disassembled carburetor. Parts were soaking in a large basin. In the middle of the garage, there was a 1977 two tone gray Dodge customized van. It had 16,000 miles on the odometer. Bobby had purchased the van off the showroom floor. It was the only new vehicle that Bobby had ever purchased.

"What do you think?" Bobby asked, beaming with pride.

"It's nice. Really nice!" Bill exclaimed, as he opened the door to look inside.

"Mary and I went to Florida in it once, but most of the time it just sits in the garage."

Mary stuck her head in the door of the garage and yelled, "That's the only thing Bobby ever bought for himself, you better take good care of it!"

"What?" For the first time in his life, Bill was at a loss for words. He was overwhelmed. The customized van still had that new car smell.

"Mary and I talked. You've always been a part of the family, and like a son to me. I want you to have this - especially since you're going straight."

"I'm going to do my best. I don't know what to say. I would've been happy driving Mary's clunker." Bill teased.

"What's the matter with my car? I like my car! It's the only Pinto I've ever seen with factory air-conditioning."

Bill and Bobby laughed heartily. They enjoyed dinner, made small talk, and the time passed quickly. Since Bill didn't have a driver's license, he would have to return to pick up the van.

The following day, Bobby dropped Bill off at the airport. It had been a great trip, one that Bill would never forget.

## CHAPTER THREE
## NEW BEGINNINGS

At the Cleveland airport Bill hailed a cab, instructing the driver to take him to the Buckeye motel. As he opened the door to his room, his attention went directly to the rubber plant with the huge elephant ears sitting in the corner. "Hello Ralph? Did you miss me? I bet you're thirsty."

After tossing his duffel bag onto the bed, he filled a plastic cup with water, gently pouring the water into the planter. Then, he dampened a wash cloth and wiped the huge leaves, one by one.

Gary was probably wondering where he had been too. It was difficult to have a conversation because he didn't want to tell anyone that he was recently released from prison. Bill had thoughtfully told Gary that his brother, Jerry, had relocated to Dayton, Ohio and himself to Cleveland to begin their new business venture, Octopool. There was no reason to tell anyone more than that.

A thought made Bill smile. He had forgotten to tell Mary that he had shopped at the Goodwill store. He doubted that she would have believed him. Mary was thoroughly disgusted at the way he wasted money. She was a penny pincher. And Bill teased that she could squeeze a quarter until the Eagle grins. At times, he would laugh and tell Mary. It's just money. They make it every day in Richmond. In hindsight, he wished that he had remembered to tell her that he had shopped at the Goodwill store.

Time passed slowly. Bill looked at his cheap Timex watch at least ten times a day. He lounged around, eating bologna sandwiches, watching TV, and at night he stayed at the Pub until closing. He admitted to himself that his cheap Timex was discoloring badly, but it still kept good time.

* * *

In the parking lot, Bill heard the sound of a horn honking. He peered through the curtains, and watched the canary yellow Cadillac Coupe Deville park. It was moving day! Bill opened the door to the motel room, smiled, and greeted Jerry and Lynn. He was excited, anxious, and ready to get the show on the road. Utilities had to be turned on, a phone connected, and furniture delivered - all in the same afternoon.

Jerry opened his trunk, and Bill tossed his duffel bag inside and closed the lid.

"Just a minute." Bill said, racing back into the room. He walked out carrying his plant, Ralph.

Lynn, sitting in the front seat, giggled, shaking her head from side to side. Jerry, on the other hand, opened the passenger door and pulled the seat forward, allowing plenty of room for the plant to sit on the backseat.

The manager of Regency Towers met them in the lobby with the keys to the apartment. Within a half hour, the furniture arrived. The truck parked at the rear exit, which was the most direct and easiest access to the apartment.

By four o'clock, the furniture was moved in, the utilities were turned on, and a phone was installed. Bill's attention now focused on all of the things that were missing. There were no linens for the bed. No blankets, no pillows. There was no towels, face clothes. There was no food in the refrigerator, or cabinets. There were no pots and pans. Not even a cup, a glass, or eating utensils. It was at this very moment the reality set in. Bill thought to himself, this is going to get expensive.

Jerry and Lynn said their goodbyes before dark. As Bill looked around the apartment, the walls were bare and there were no curtains covering the windows. He had no TV, no radio, and he was left alone with his thoughts. Bill walked to the Kroger's Supermarket and bought the necessities to get through the night. Towels, wash clothes, and several rolls of toilet paper. Directly across the street from Kroger's was a Kentucky Fried Chicken. He purchased a bucket of chicken, large fries, and a two liter of Pepsi-Cola.

Returning to the apartment, Bill called Lee's apartment. There was no answer. So, he sat down at the kitchen table and ate. It would be nice if he had a glass, or even a paper plate he told himself. After dinner, he showered and tried to get some sleep. But the calmness was overwhelming. There had to be something to do! Then, he thought of the Ground Round. There was a horseshoe bar in a room opposite the dining room where he, Jerry and Lynn, had eaten. The smell of popcorn had drawn his attention to the bar. Just inside the doorway there was a red and yellow popcorn machine.

Bill dressed, deciding on a dark blue pin-stripe suit that he had purchased at the Goodwill store. He left the apartment through the front foyer. It was a nice night for a walk, warm, with a gentle breeze, and the sidewalks were well lighted. He crossed the street, walked a block past the Kentucky Fried Chicken to the Ground Round. The parking lot was filled with cars, and people were walking in and out of the double doors at the entrance. As Bill walked inside, he saw the popcorn machine. He stood at the entrance to the bar for a minute to allow his eyes to adjust. There were tables with red and white checkered table cloths and a long bar in the shape of a half -moon with barstools. As Bill was making his decision someone shouted,

"Hey! Get a look at this guy!" At the same time, Bill was bombarded with a was handful of peanut shells. The patrons were laughing heartily. As Bill looked around the bar he spotted the culprit sitting on a barstool at the far end of the counter, grinning like the Cheshire Cat. About every four feet there was a basket of peanuts on top of the counter. The culprit responsible for the devious act was wearing a yellow short sleeve shirt with an impressive multi-colored gold chain that lay flat to his neck. He had coal black hair and a rounded face. Bill grabbed a handful of peanuts, took aim, and threw them.

"Hey! This guy's alright. Give him a drink on me." Bill's half-inebriated assailant introduced himself as Bobby Hardin, laughed, and told Bill that he was overdressed for the Ground Round. The night ended with the bar closing, and a lonely walk back to an empty apartment.

* * *

After dialing Lee's number more than a dozen times, there was finally an answer.

"It's your dime." Lee said.

"I thought you were in jail."

"No." Lee sighed. "I've been busy. Yesterday I had to sell my Corvette.

It was either that, or starve."

"That bad, huh?"

"I'm sure I've had better days, but I really can't remember when."

"I moved to the apartment yesterday. But I never realized how much stuff that I was going to need. The list just keeps growing. Lee, I don't have curtains covering my windows. Nor do I have a radio, much less a TV."

"That's pretty sad." Lee admitted.

The room was so empty. There was nothing at all. Absolutely nothing! It was at that very moment Bill realized what he was missing. And the second Lee hung up, Bill called Jerry.

"Hello?" Lynn answered.

"Ugh. Is Jerry, by any chance, at home?"

"May I ask whose calling?" Lynn knew damn well who was calling. Her asking made her Jerry's accomplice!

"Tell Jerry that I received the ransom demand."

"You must be mistaken." Jerry laughed, taking the phone from Lynn. "There's been no ransom demand."

"I want Ralph back!"

Jerry laughed so hard his belly hurt. "We were halfway home when Lynn looked in the backseat and realized that you had abandoned Ralph."

"You kidnapped my friggin plant!"

"I did no such thing."

Bill and Jerry exchanged words like great warriors, then Bill relented, admitting they deserved something for their taking excellent care of Ralph.

That night Bill wore jeans and a long sleeve shirt to the Ground Round. Bill rarely wore short sleeve shirts because he felt people, as a general rule, placed people with tattoos in a less desirable category. And he wanted to rub elbows with the upper class. He felt that he could learn from people who were focused and successful.

Bobby Hardin was already at the Ground Round when Bill arrived. Like himself, Bobby was single and lived alone. He was dating one of the barmaids, off and on. This was one of their on nights and Bobby was generously buying drinks for everyone seated at the bar. As Bill and Bobby talked, they learned more about each other. They both lived at Regency Towers, just in different buildings. Bobby lived one building to the right of Bill on the third floor. He had lived at Regency Towers for three years. Bobby owned a small trucking company and hauled local freight. He worked hard, and he played hard. On Saturday night he invited a few close friends to his apartment for a poker game, and he invited Bill. After closing the Ground Round, Bobby had noticed Bill walking back to the apartments and thoughtfully asked if he had a car?

"My license is suspended, but I have a 1977 customized Dodge van sitting in a garage in Maryland."

At closing, Bobby wanted to leave with his girlfriend, the barmaid. He had rode his motorcycle to the Ground Round, so he asked Bill if he would ride his motorcycle back to the apartments, and he would pick it up the next day.

"I don't have a license." Bill reminded Bobby.

"You're not planning on getting caught, are you?" Bobby chuckled.

"No!" Bill replied, more as a matter of fact. They exchanged phone numbers, and Bobby left with his girlfriend. The motorcycle was a 1974 Honda 125cc with a four speed transmission. At closing, Bobby walked Bill to where he had parked his motorcycle, handed him the keys, and they parted company. It was a warm night and the short ride to the apartment felt good - especially good to someone who had been locked up for several years. It was a feeling of freedom. Total freedom! A warm wind rustled through his hair and his shirt blew in the wind. The ride was nice, but much too short. Normally Bill used the front entrance, but tonight he rode past the front foyer, turned left, and parked the Honda in the rear parking lot. He walked through the exit door, turned the key to unlock the door of his apartment, and a rush of cool air struck him squarely in the face. He relished the thought that things were getting better. As he flipped on a light switch, his eyes fell upon the barren room. There was definitely not a feeling of coming home, not yet anyway.

Bill opened the refrigerator, grabbed the half-empty bucket of chicken and what was left of the two liter of Pepsi-Cola. Then he sat down at the kitchen table, and ate. He thought about planning his day for tomorrow. The thought brought a quick grin to his face, there was nothing to plan!

* * *

Bill awoke to the sound of silence. It was a strange feeling, something he was not familiar with. In prison, the slightest sound would have been an eye opener. There was a jingling of the guard's keys when they made rounds. An alarm clock, the flushing of a toilet. Things that were heard, but slept through. To wake up to silence was just plain weird.

As if by ritual, when he crawled out of bed he stopped to tuck the sheets in and fluff the pillows. But there were none. He walked to the bathroom, showered, then stood looking at himself in the mirror. It was nice to look at himself in a real mirror, he thought. Remembering the little plastic square mirrors sold in the prisoner store. He could barely see himself in those. Through bitter experience, he had learned not to take anything for granted and to appreciate the things he had, which wasn't much he reminded himself with a chuckle. He dressed, and left the apartment. It was time to buy some real groceries. Once inside Krogers, he grabbed a shopping cart and walked up and down the aisles turning his head in both directions.

He was tempted by everything, but he would not be foolish. He would only purchase things he needed. Now, he understood why women made shopping lists. Flying by the seat of his britches wasn't one of his better ideas. He rationalized that he wasn't going to be cooking because there were no pots and pans. With that in mind, he purchased items that needed very little preparation. He splurged buying paper plates, plastic forks, spoons, knives, and cups. He added napkins, soap, shampoo, and a Rubbermaid trash can with some plastic liners. Then, he bought orange juice, one two liter of Pepsi-Cola, bread, butter, peanut butter, jelly, tuna fish, mayonnaise, ketchup, and mustard. From the frozen food department he bought a pizza and some TV dinners. He purchased aspirin, an alarm clock, and a two slice toaster that was on sale.

As Bill pushed the shopping cart to the apartment he learned to lift the front of the cart, then the back, when he had to go over a curb. The front wheels wobbled, and with every crevice in the sidewalk he could hear and feel a thud.

Bobby's Honda was still parked at the curb in the rear parking lot. Thank God no one had stolen it! He thought about going for a ride, but Bobby had only given him permission to ride it back to Regency Towers.

As Bill reached to unlock the exit door, he looked over his right shoulder. There was a gathering of beautiful girls sunbathing. They were laying on beach towels on a concrete slab in front of the Community Center and indoor pool.

Bill looked at his cheap Timex watch, it was ten o' clock in the morning. Inside the apartment, he quickly put the groceries away, dropped the cart off in the rear parking lot, and walked to the Parma Mall. It was a massive indoor Mall with stores as far as the eye could see. In the middle of the Mall, there were displays, water fountains, benches, and eateries with tables. Poles with chains set up the perimeter for each area. An escalator moved shoppers from one floor to the next. The upstairs was open with a windowed ceiling allowing light to shine through. Bill marveled at the architect's ability to create such a magnificent structure. Shoppers on the upper level stopped and leaned against the brass railings to watch the movement below. Bill walked by a movie theater, a pet store, and more shoe stores than he cared to count. This Mall had everything, including a florist. There were candy stores, clothing stores with the latest women's fashions, while others sold men's suits and apparel. The store Wet and Wild had mannequins in the window wearing bathing suits.

Ten minutes later, with his purchase of bathing trunks and a beach towel he began the walk back to his apartment. On his way, he stopped at a State Liquor store and purchased a fifth of Seagram's Seven, a two liter of Seven-Up, and a bag of crushed ice.

Back at the apartment, Bill made himself a drink and tried on his new bathing trunks. They were a pattern of red, white, and blue. He stood in front of a full length mirror that hung on the back of the door to his walk-in closet. His legs were noticeably white. He was embarrassed by his lack of a tan, and of his tattoos as well. He tried to find the courage to overcome that, one drink at a time. It was barely noon.

In the kitchen, he opened the box containing the toaster, placed it on the kitchen counter and plugged it in. It was the one luxury that he had allowed himself. He opened a loaf of bread, placed two slices in the toaster, and pressed the lever down. He watched as the bread disappeared and the coils slowly glowed red. Within seconds, the smell of browning bread filled the air.

Bill opened the jar of mayonnaise, grabbed a can of tuna fish, and cursed. He hadn't thought to buy a can opener. When the toast popped up, he ate it raw.

## CHAPTER FOUR
## THE ROUNDABOUT

Two months later the solitude, loneliness, and frustrations were taking their toll. Bobby Hardin introduced Bill to the bank manager at Dollar bank, Vaughn Medcalf. The branch Vaughn managed for in the same Plaza as Kroger's supermarket. Vaughn played cards weekly at Bobby's apartment and he told Bill that he could authorize up to a $5,000 personal loan without his having to ask for authorization from the Board of Director's. Bill wanted to obtain a $3500 loan using the 1977 customized Dodge van as collateral. Vaughn assured Bill that would be no problem.

Bill needed for Bobby to ask Mary if he could use their license tag and insurance to drive the van to Ohio, but he still hadn't found the right time to discuss things with Mary. She had grown up in Savage, Maryland, a small town nearly twenty miles from where they now lived. Mary's family was so poor she had one pair of shoes, which she was only allowed to wear to school and church. Bill still remembered the time he went grocery shopping with Mary. As he pushed the cart, she opened her purse, grabbed a handful of coupons, and began tossing grocery items into the cart explaining, Mary had always commented on how wasteful Bill was of money, and that made her sick to her stomach.

When Bill talked to his friends, his favorite saying was that he was on the roundabout. When asked what that meant, he grinned and replied "Round about the time that I get things together I'm going to be flat broke!"

Bobby Hardin didn't say it, but he was beginning to doubt that Bill had a customized van in a garage in Maryland, and he was regretting telling Bill to keep the motorcycle until he picked up the van.

Lee Chambers was calling every day. He didn't want to pay for another months rent, so he was selling everything he could, donating the rest to Goodwill, and planning to fly to Ohio that weekend having already purchased his one-way ticket.

\* \* \*

From the Cleveland International Airport, Lee hailed a cab giving directions to Regency Towers in Parma Heights. With him, he had forty-two hundred dollars in cash and whatever he could fit into two suitcases.

When Lee buzzed the apartment from the front foyer, Bill pressed the button allowing him entry, then rushed to meet Lee in the Lobby.

"Welcome to Ohio." Bill smiled, grabbing one of the suitcases. "Did you have a good flight?"

"It was okay, if you like flying." Lee stuttered. He was half drunk, that was obvious by his impaired speech.

"Follow me." Bill said, leading the way. The apartment was at the end of the hallway on the right. Bill had purchased drapes for the living room window, curtains for his bedroom, and hung two wooden glassed candle holders on the wall.

"Welcome to my humble abode." Bill grinned, closing the door behind them. After giving Lee the fifty cent tour of the apartment, Bill opened the door to Lee's bedroom. There were no curtains, much less a bed.

Lee chuckled and asked. "Where am I supposed to sleep?"

"I guess on the couch until we can find a bed for you."

"Works for me." Lee countered.

"Are you hungry?"

"Starved!"

"Well, would you like to freshen up first, or do you want to go get something to eat?"

"What part of starved didn't you understand?"

They left through the front foyer walking three blocks to the Ground Round.

Bill told Lee the U.S. Marshals provided him with a new Social Security card and said they could not help with a drivers license because his license was revoked in the state of Tennessee.

"I've never lived in the State of Tennessee." Bill added, before asking Lee if he had a birth certificate.

"Of course, I do." Lee grinned.

"Would you mind if I copied it, whited-out your name and birth date, then made a Birth Certificate for myself?"

"I don't care." Lee replied as they neared the Ground Round.

Once inside the Ground Round, they ordered sandwiches and drinks. It was mid afternoon with very few customers.

"I've gotta tell you, nothing about Ohio has impressed me yet!" Lee grinned at his friend.

"Give it some time, it will grow on you."

At four-thirty Bobby Hardin walked into the bar. At five o' clock there was a free buffet and fried chicken wings were the special of the day, his favorite. Bill introduced Lee to his newest friend, Bobby. The pair quickly exchanged jokes at the expense of Bill, then Bobby ordered a round of drinks.

\* \* \*

The next morning, Lee unpacked and showed Bill his birth certificate. It was perfect. Bill was sure that he could whiteout the name and date without distorting the lines. After a quick shower and shave, he set out on his mission riding the Honda to an Office Supply store where he purchased a bottle of white-out. Then he went to the Parma Library, with, a copy of the birth certificate, whiting-out Lee's name and birth date. He made a copy of the blank birth certificate, then typed in William Daniel Burns with his birthdate December 3, 1947. He copied the typed certificate. As he inspected the document, he smiled, sure that it would pass any inspection!

With his birth certificate and new Social Security card in hand, Bill's next stop was at the Department of Motor Vehicles where he obtained an Ohio driver's license.

As Bill entered the apartment, he flashed his new driver's license at Lee.

Lee grinned, then asked. "How did you manage that trick?"

"I copied your birth certificate, whited out your name and birthdate and typed mine in." Bill replied flatly, grinning from ear to ear.

That night Bill called Bobby Jenkins to let him know that he would be there on the weekend to pick up the van. Then, he called Jerry and he reported that Richard had called and said there's a good chance of his being released earlier than expected, which was good news. Jerry had built a prototype, but they were depending on Richard for the refinancing to put the wheels in motion. Richard knew bankers and investors!

"How's Ralph?" Bill chuckled.

"He's living a life of luxury." Jerry replied.

Bill told Jerry about the weeks events. Lee moved in. He had forged a birth certificate, got his driver's license and was flying to Maryland Friday night to pick up the customized van.

That weekend Bill flew to Maryland, picked up the van, and drove it back to Ohio.

Monday night Bill drove the van to the Ground Round to show it off to Bobby Hardin and his banker friend, Vaughn Medcalf. Vaughn told Bill to stop by anytime during the week and he would fill out the paperwork for the loan.

After a hard night of partying, the next morning Bill prepared himself to go to the Dollar bank and meet with Vaughn. As he parked the van, he looked at the large rectangular blue, white, and yellow neon sign above the building, it simply read DOLLAR BANK. Instinctively, as Bill entered the glass double doors his eye's swept the room - as if he was casing the bank to rob it. Directly ahead of him was a counter with four tellers. Behind the counter was a hallway with rooms on both sides, and an exit door.

Stepping up to the counter, Bill asked a female clerk for the bank manager, Vaughn Medcalf. She picked up a phone and buzzed his office which was partitioned off near the front entrance. Vaughn stepped out, smiled, and waved Bill to his office.

Bill seated himself in a brown cushioned chair as Vaughn asked. "What can I do for you today?"

"First, I would like to start by using the Dodge van as security for a $3500 loan. Secondly, I want to open a checking and savings account. And third, if it's possible, I would like to get a secured Master and Visa card."

"Do you have any credit now?"

"No. I've always paid cash for whatever I purchased."

"I would suggest that you set a balance on the Visa and Master card at $500. The amount of the security is your limit. So, both cards will have a five hundred dollar limit at a cost to you of $1,000."

"That will work fine for me."

After Bill filled out the credit information, when Vaughn inspected it, he asked why there was no prior history? No previous addresses, and no prior work record.

"I've always worked for myself."

"How do you want the money distributed?"

"Put $1000. in savings, and $1,000. in my checking account, and give me $500 in cash."

Bill signed the paperwork, handed Vaughn the title to the van, so that he could put the lien on the title, and Vaughn handed Bill $500. in cash, a copy of the loan contract, and receipts. "You should receive the credit cards and checks in the mail within the next two weeks," Vaughn concluded.

It was a beautiful day! As Bill stepped from the bank, the warmth of the sun wrapped around him like a warm blanket. He squinted his eyes to protect them from the glaring sun. He decided to take a drive to the Lamp Light to see his friendly bartender, Gary. As Bill pulled up in front of the Pub, Gary was sweeping the sidewalk.

"Did you find a place?" Gary asked, as Bill stepped out of the van.

"Sure did. I rented an apartment at Regency Towers. Are you open yet?"

"We're open for business!" Gary quickly pointed out. "Is that your van?"

As they walked inside the Pub, the coolness of the air-conditioning felt good.

"Yes, that's my van. I just went to Maryland and picked it up this past weekend." Bill replied, ordering a Seven and Seven along with a steak sandwich and fries.

After chatting for the better part of an hour, Gary suggested that on his way back to Parma Heights he take the scenic route through the park.

A winding road swerved through the evergreen forest. There was freshly mowed grass, picnic tables, streams, and a directory pointing the way to stables, a swimming area, and walking trails. Visitors cooked on grills while others polished their treasured cars beneath shade trees.

Arriving back at the apartment Bill felt that it was beginning to feel like home.

Later that night, Bill told Lee about the plans for the future to build Octopool. "It's an eight-men Jacuzzi with powerful jets. There's nothing like it on the market and because it becomes a permanent fixture in the house, it qualifies for a Home Improvement Loan."

"How did you come up with this idea?"

"A guy that I met in prison, Jerry Burns, drew up the Plans. Upon his release, he relocated to Dayton, Ohio along with his girlfriend, Lynn Bailey. And with their help, I relocated to Cleveland. Jerry went to work selling swimming pools and he has made a prototype of the spa. Our logo is an Octopus climbing out of a champagne glass. Another guy, Richard Biggerstaff will be released in the next few months. Richard knows wealthy people. Bankers and investors who will invest in the business."

"It sounds like a great idea, but it's hard for me to think of you of anything other than a bank robber." Lee chuckled.

"Better get used to it." Bill smiled.

* * *

Thursday morning Bill crawled out of bed, looked at the alarm clock seeing the time was half past eleven. Rubbing the sleep from his eyes, he yawned, then crawled out of the bed performing his daily rituals. He made the bed, showered, dressed, put two slices of bread into the toaster and pressed the lever down. That would be his breakfast! He thought to himself that it was going to take time getting use to the rented waterbed, especially after a night of heavy drinking.

In his bedroom there was a waterbed that had a wooden headboard with a shelf and a nitelight for reading. On both sides of the headboard were narrow shelves with glass sliding doors. He guessed they were bookshelves. There was a five drawer dresser, a night stand with a clock and phone, and lamp, and a huge walk in closet. He kept the door to the closet closed because there was very little in it.

Bill and Lee left the apartment deciding to check-out the indoor swimming pool and community clubhouse. The concrete slab in front of the indoor pool was topped with blankets, beach towels, and sunbathers. Mostly attractive girl's in string bikinis. Inside the building there was a weight room with an indoor sauna and lockers.

As they stepped back into the sunlight, Lee grinned admiring the bathing beauties. If he missed his wife and kids, it wasn't at the moment. While Bill thought of his daughters, his son, and with all of his heart and his every being he wished that he could change his past. He knew that was something he could never do, but surely there were better days ahead.

# CHAPTER FIVE
## BETTER DAYS

Bill tried unsuccessfully to call Bobby several times throughout the day. He walked to Krogers purchasing one item, a can opener. Returning to the apartment he toasted two slices of bread and made two tuna fish sandwiches, serving himself on a paper plate with a handful of Lay's potato chips. It was a huge improvement over bologna sandwiches, he mused.

That evening when Bill walked into the Ground Round Bobby was seated in his usual place at the bar, laughing, and having a good time.

"I've been trying to call. You're a hard person to catch." Bill grinned.

"That's because I haven't been home." Bobby chuckled, and looked at his girlfriend behind the bar. She looked up at Bill, and smiled.

"Well, your motorcycle is parked behind my building. I don't need it now that I have my van."

"Okay." Bobby grinned.

"Give Bill a drink!" He told the barmaid.

She looked at Bill.

"Seven and Seven, sweetheart." Bill answered the look on her face.

"I've got a name, and it's not sweetheart."

"I'm sure you do, but we've never been properly introduced. Let's start over. Hi! My name is Bill, and you are?"

"Sandy," she smiled.

"Well Sandy. May I please have a Seven and Seven?"

"It's on the way."

"By the way, Billy." Bobby chimed in. "There's going to be a poker game at my apartment tomorrow night if you and Lee would like to come? It's nothing big. Just quarter dollar."

"What time. And what is your apartment number?"

"We usually start around eight and my apartment number is really easy to remember 4-1-1. Just like dialing information!"

"Count me in."

"I hope I'm not inviting a card shark." Bobby chuckled, adding. "This is a game among friends."

* * *

Friday night at seven forty-five Bill stood in the foyer of Bobby Hardin's apartment building looking at the directory. Next to last name Hardin 411 was a round black button. He pressed it. The foyer door buzzed, and over the intercom Bobby said "C'mon up!"

The lobby wasn't nearly as nicely furnished as the building Bill lived in, and there was less decor. Bill took the elevator to the fourth floor. As he stepped out, the hallway was barren, not a person in sight. The apartment doors were numbered and went higher to the right. Bobby's apartment was midway down on the left facing the front parking lot. Bill knocked lightly on the door and Bobby answered it with a warm smile and a firm handshake inviting him inside. At a glance, Bill noticed the apartment, although a bachelor pad, was tastefully decorated. Centered in the living room was a big screen TV in a cherry cabinet. A gray sectional pit group with a white bear skin rug beneath a coffee table with matching end tables filled the room. A large painting in a gold frame hung on a wall, and two rectangular mirrors were thoughtfully hung on another wall. Unlike his own apartment, Bobby's was well furnished and smelled fresh. Two men were already seated at the dining room table with drinks in their hands. Bill immediately recognized one of the men, Vaughn Medcalf. He was in his mid thirties wearing a suit and tie. Vaughn had short brown hair, neatly combed, and stood about five feet eight.

Bobby introduced the second man as, Carl. He was a huge black man dressed in blue jeans, and a white tee shirt with bulging muscles. Carl was well groomed, mild mannered, and his teeth were pearl white. He stood up, extended his hand in friendship, and said. "Nice to meet you." His grip was firm and Bill was pleased when the gentle giant let go of his hand after two short friendly shakes.

"What are you drinking, Billy?" Bobby asked.

"Seven and Seven."

"How about Jack Daniels and Seven, or" he named off several other bourbons.

"Black Velvet would be fine?"

"Carl drives a truck for me." Bobby offered.

"What kind of work do you do?" Carl asked Bill.

"I'm currently unemployed. I recently moved to Cleveland for a business venture. My brother and I plan to market an eight men Jacuzzi, Octopool."

"Good luck with that, Bill. Let me know when the spa goes on the market."

"I'll be your first customer." Bobby offered, then asked. "Is Lee coming?"

"No, he doesn't gamble."

"I invited a couple of other guys, but let's get started. If they show up, they show up." Bobby concluded.

Bill won forty-two dollars. Towards the end of the night, Bobby asked if he would give him a hand moving a girl from Regency Towers to a house that she was renting with two other girls. "Dottie lives across the hall from me."

"When do you want to start?"

"Not too early. I'm thinking around ten o'clock in the morning. She's not attractive to me. Dottie is just a really nice girl and I offered to help her out!"

"Give me a call when you're ready."

The next morning Bill called Bobby Jenkins informing him that the van would be going into his name Monday. Bobby was happy to hear that, and asked. "Did I tell you what Mary said when I asked her if you could drive the van to Ohio using our tags and insurance?"

"I don't recall your telling me."

"I figured that after a few drinks she would be a better mood. She placed both hands on my chest and shoved me backwards hard. Then, she glared at me and announced, 'You aren't slick!' She went from feeling tipsy to being as sober as a church mouse. Then she giggled and told me to tell you that you'd better be careful."

Bill laughed at just how smart Mary was.

At ten o' clock Bobby called, he was at the apartment with one of his cube trucks.

"Give me ten minutes." Bill replied.

When Bill arrived, Bobby was carrying boxes to the freight elevator stacking them one on top of another. "Want a beer?" he offered.

"Sure!" Bill popped the top from a can of Budweiser and asked why Bobby wasn't using the shopping carts at the rear of the building.

"Great idea!" Bobby grinned. Minutes later they were racing shopping carts filled with Dottie's treasures down the carpeted hallway.

Dottie was short, didn't appear to be beyond thirty. She had short brown hair, a mole on her left cheek, and she was seriously overweight. Her lease was up, and shared expenses with two other girls was going to be cheaper.

After the truck was loaded, Dottie made one final inspection to make sure nothing was left behind. Then, they followed her five miles to the rental house. Bobby had thoughtfully grabbed a six pack of beer from his refrigerator. With his right arm, Bill wiped the sweat from his forehead. He wasn't accustomed to hard labor, and it showed. He popped a top from a can of beer and guzzled half of it to quench his thirst.

Fifteen minutes later, Dottie pulled into the driveway of a small white house, then drove off into the grass, giving Bobby a hand gesture to wait a minute as she disappeared inside the house. Less than a minute later, Dottie returned with one of the other girl's who moved her car out of the driveway. Bobby backed the truck into the driveway. Behind the house was a huge field of grass with a baseball diamond. Dottie's bed room was just inside the side door, to the left of the kitchen.

Dottie introduced Bobby and Bill to her roommates. Karen was five-seven, medium size, with long brown hair. Her boyfriend and a couple of his buddies were there to help the girls move. Bonnie was a striking brunette, with a smile that lit-up the room. From the moment Bill and Bonnie met, there was a chemistry and instant attraction.

"Can I borrow him for a minute?" Bonnie asked Dottie, nodding in

Bill's direction, smiling.

Dottie knew damn well Bonnie could have asked someone else for help.

Bonnie's room was in the basement. In fact, she had the entire basement to herself. She asked Bill to stack some hats on a shelf in her bed room closet, offering a chair for him to stand on, then she stood behind him. "Where did you meet Dottie?" she asked.

"I'm new to the area. The first person I met was Bobby Hardin. I walked into the Ground Round in Parma wearing a suit. He threw a handful of peanuts at me, so I grabbed a handful and threw them back at him. He laughed, bought me a drink, and that's how our friendship began. There was a poker game at his apartment last night. He asked if I would give him a hand moving a girl from Regency Towers to a house today. I said that I would, and, well - here I am!"

"Would you care for another beer?" Bonnie offered.

"Sure." Bill smiled.

With cold beers in hand they walked outside, sat down at a picnic table beneath a huge shade tree and they talked. Bonnie was a Home Economics teacher at a High School in Brecksville. A prestigious area, where wealthy people lived. When they were out of beer, Bonnie asked if he wanted to take a ride with her to the store?

Dottie stepped from the house, and yelled. "I told you that you could borrow him, not keep him!"

Bonnie laughed, ushering Bill in to her car. The car was nine years old. It was a 1970 metallic brown Chevrolet Malibu convertible rusting badly around the rear fender wells, dinged on the right front fender, and the raggedy black convertible top was held together by gray duck tape. it had black sidewall tires with no hub caps. The day was warm, so Bonnie flipped the latches, pressed a button under the dash, and the top folded back like an accordion. As she started the engine it became blatantly obvious the car was in need of a new muffler too. As she pulled out of the driveway, Bonnie mentioned she needed to make a quick stop by her old apartment to make sure nothing was left behind. At a nearby convenient store she stopped and purchased a six pack of Budweiser. Her old apartment was less than a mile away in a complex on the second floor. The apartment faced the rear of the building and a wooden porch allowed a view of the woods. Once inside the apartment, Bonnie opened the door to the porch and stepped outside. Bill followed, leaning against a railing he took note of his surroundings. The lawn was recently mowed and the woods were less than fifty feet from the building. They sat down on the porch, drank beer, and talked for at least forty-five minutes before deciding they should be getting back. Bonnie quickly ran from room to room checking to make sure there was nothing left behind, then locked the door behind them. As they drove back to the house, she invited Bill to her house next weekend for an appreciation cookout.

\* \* \*

Throughout the week Bill thought about Bonnie, and wondered if she had been thinking about him too. Bonnie was 'hot' and they seemed to have a lot in-common. It felt good being with Bonnie. It felt Right! Bill wished he had thought to ask for her phone number. How stupid could he be? What an idiot, he thought.

At the picnic there was barbequed chicken, pork chops, and ribs. The picnic table was covered with a red and white checkerboard plastic table cloth. On top of the table were bowls of potato salad, coleslaw, baked beans, and corn on the cob. For dessert there were homemade pies, apple and peach. And there was a double layer chocolate cake with chocolate icing.

Dottie had told Bonnie the story of Bobby loaning Bill his Honda when he didn't have transportation, adding that Bill was now driving a two-tone gray customized van. When Bonnie saw a gray van approaching she ran into the house and looked in the mirror making sure that she looked her best.

As Bill parked, Bonnie nonchalantly strolled out of the house to greet him. Smiling, she took him by the hand introducing Bill to all of her friends, one by one. It was clear, he was with Bonnie! She waited on him hand and foot, making sure his plate was full and he always had a cold beer. Bill was being spoiled rotten, and loving every minute of it.

Before nightfall, they were walking around arm in arm displaying signs of affection. They kissed and exchanged phone numbers when it was time to say goodbye.

* * *

Back at the apartment Bill told Lee about Bonnie. And Lee told Bill about the love of his life, Jenny. She had left him because he couldn't hold down a job. He liked to stay up late and none of his employers had been understanding of his constantly showing up late for work. After being fired from his last job, Jenny was fed up with his bullshit. Lee said that he missed his wife and kids, and more than anything in the world he wanted them back. He had sold his Corvette because he didn't want to take the risk of his going to prison. From the moment he had heard that Bill was going straight, he knew that he didn't want to miss the opportunity to be a part of that.

Bonnie called, volunteering to come over and help Bill organize his apartment. Bill had no pots and pans or dishes, so he and Bonnie went shopping. Bonnie was a conservative shopper, only buying items on sale. Since she helped Bill, he promised to hang some things in her house the following day.

CHAPTER SIX
MOVING ON UP


Bonnie wasn't sure if Bill would be thoughtful enough to call if their plans had changed. Tormented by the thought that something may have unexpectedly come up, she looked for a reason to call him. Desperate, she picked up the phone and dialed his apartment.

"Hello?" Bill answered on the third ring.

"Hi! This is Bonnie," she began. "Will you be here in time for lunch, and is Lee coming with you?"

"Yes, and no." Bill quickly answered.

"Would you like breakfast, or lunch?"

"Either will be fine. Whatever's the easiest for you."

"Do you know anything about cars?" Bonnie asked, changing the subject. "Mine started making a funny sound on my way home yesterday."

"I'll take a look at it."

At one o'clock Bill pulled into Bonnie's driveway and parked. There were no other cars, other than Bonnie's Malibu parked in the grass beneath a huge oak tree. Dottie and Karen were both at work. One of the perks of being a teacher were when the students were off, so were the teachers.

When Bill arrived, the first thing he asked for were the keys to Bonnie's car. She walked outside with him. As he lifted the hood, he checked the oil. It was more than a quart low. Then, he told Bonnie to 'start the engine.' The power steering belt made a loud screeching sound.

"That's the noise!" Bonnie shouted. "Shut the engine off."

Bill walked inside the house and grabbed a bar of soap off the kitchen counter. Then he felt the power steering belt to see if it was loose. It wasn't.

"Start the engine."

As the belt turned, he soaped the edge of the belt until it stopped squealing.

"How do you like your eggs?" Bonnie smiled, as they walked into the house.

"Sunny side up." Bill said, returning her smile.

Bonnie made four slices of toast, buttered them, then sat a jar of strawberry jelly on the table.

"Coffee, or orange juice?" She offered.

"Do you have any Pepsi-Cola?"

"Pepsi-Cola with breakfast? Yuck! How can you drink that with breakfast?"

"It's good!" Bill chuckled.

"There's an Auto Parts store at the corner. While you enjoy your breakfast, I'll make a quick trip to pick up a quart of oil."

As Bonnie hurried to her car, Bill yelled. "Ask if they have any muffler bearings while your there!"

Five minutes later Bonnie returned, slamming her car door she rushed into the house, stood in front of Bill with her hands on her hips, and shouted. "There's no such thing as muffler bearings, is there? One of the guys asked what color I wanted while another said that he thought they were out of stock. Everyone in the store was laughing!"

Bill grinned. After hanging pictures in the living room and putting up a shelf for spices in the kitchen, he left. Bonnie blessed him with a long, well deserved, passionate kiss.

When Bill returned to the apartment, Lee waived to him from the clubhouse. As Bill parked, Lee walked to meet him. "Did you know that there's party rooms in every building that can be rented? After nine o'clock at night you can rent the entire clubhouse and indoor pool."

"That's nice." Bill grinned.

Thursday night Bill called and invited Bonnie to go to Dayton with him for the weekend. He wanted to introduce her to his brother Jerry and his girlfriend, Lynn.

Friday night he picked Bonnie up at her house. She packed an overnight bag, and stocked a cooler with snacks and beverages - even though it was only a two hour drive. Seventy-five North was a direct route to Dayton, Ohio. When they exited the highway, Jerry's directions were to make a right. However, to the left there was a Comfort Inn and Bill decided to check-in there first. While Bonnie primped, he called Jerry suggesting the four of them go out for dinner. Bill was anxious to show off his new van.

"Steak and lobster it is then." Jerry quipped.

Everyone dressed casual. Bonnie and Lynn wore slacks and nice blouses. Jerry wore black slacks with a white turtle neck sweater. And Bill wore blue slacks with a short sleeve yellow knit shirt.

Bonnie and Lynn were sitting in the rear of the van while Bill and Jerry sat in the Captain chairs discussing their plans for Octopool. A song came over the radio "...wouldn't it be nice if we could wake up..."

"Who sings that?" Bonnie asked.

"The Temptations!" Bill replied, continuing his conversation with Jerry.

A half mile farther down the road, Jerry corrects Bill. "That's not who sings that song, it's The Beach Boys!"

Bill smiled, and replied. "She was perfectly content with my answer."

Bonnie playfully thumped Bill in the back of his head, laughed, and said. "You liar!"

At the restaurant the girls drank wine, while Bill and Jerry ordered Crown Royal on the rocks. A good time was enjoyed by all.

Returning to Jerry's he insisted they come upstairs for a nightcap. The apartment was small but nicely decorated. There wasn't a dirty dish, a crumb on the floor, or anything that looked out of place. In the corner, next to the curtains that opened to a sliding glass door that led to a concrete balcony was Ralph. The plant was looking much larger and greener. Bill picked up the plant, Jerry stood on the opposite side of Bill, and Bonnie took a photo of Jerry, Ralph, and Bill.

In the living room on a shelf near the door was a ceramic statue of W. C. Fields. When it was time to leave, on his way out the door, Bill snatched it!

Bill and Bonnie spent the night together at the Comfort Inn, returning to Cleveland Saturday afternoon. After dropping Bonnie off at her house, Bill returned to the apartment.

* * *

Sunday morning, Bill picked up a local newspaper and thumbed through the Help Wanted Ads, one page at a time. He was running low on money. An ad caught his eye. Executive International Development Corporation at 1440 Snow Road was interviewing for sales representatives. Call Gary Archdeacon between 8 a.m. and 4 p.m. Monday through Friday. Bill quickly wrote the phone number on a piece of paper and placed it next to the phone in his bedroom. The first thing Monday morning, he called the number and the secretary referred him to the Vice President, Don Conley. Bill made an appointment to interview at 10 a.m. Wednesday.

Wednesday morning Bill dressed in his blue pin-stripe suit. He wore a light blue shirt open at the collar because he didn't own a tie. He looked respectful, he thought, standing in front of the mirror.

At nine forty-five Bill parked in front of the rectangular red brick building. As he walked inside, to his right there was a glass cabinet with a directory. Against a black board white lettering read EXECUTIVE INTERNATIONAL DEVELOPMENT CORPORATION, first floor room 100. The door was clearly marked, and it was the first door on the left. As Bill opened the door, the receptionist desk was directly in front of him. She smiled welcoming Bill, and her name tag read Celeste. She buzzed Don Conley's office announcing that his ten o'clock appointment was there, then politely asked if she could get him a cup of coffee.

"No, thank you." Bill smiled, sitting down in a chair. He picked a magazine from a rack and browsed through it. Before he had time to decide on an article, Don stepped out of his office, extended his hand to greet him, and grinned broadly.

Don Conley was short, balding, well dressed, and wore gold horn-rimmed designer glasses. Don's blue pin stripe suit was a three piece. Slacks, vest, and jacket. His long sleeve silk shirt was complemented by a dark tie, a solid gold tie bar, and gold cuff links. On his left wrist he wore a gold watch. On his right, a thick gold link chain. One thing for certain, Don Conley dressed to impress. As Bill followed Don to his office, they walked passed a curved wall covered in silver patterned wallpaper that shined to a high gloss. It was the first curved wall he had ever seen, and very impressive. Entering Don's office, he motioned Bill to have a seat in a cushioned chair opposite his desk. On his desk were framed family photos, a globe of the world that spun on a wooden base, and numerous diplomas that hung neatly on the wall. Next to the door there was a wooden hat rack with brass hangers. Don's matching suit jacket hung on a hook, and a dress hat with the brim turned slightly down hung on another. Bill looked at the cuff of his suit and hoped his cheap Timex watch or tattoos hadn't been exposed.

Don began the interview by asking if he had any sales experience? Bill had sold magazines door to door and sewing machines when he worked at Frank Kalita's store, Stitch and Save. But he opted not to mention either.

"No!" Bill replied flatly.

"It doesn't matter. The corporation has their own training program." Don offered.

The owner and President, Gary Archdeacon, stepped into Don's office, extended his hand, and introduced himself. Gary was in his late forties, of average build, and he also wore a dark blue pin-stripe suit. His shoes were a soft leather Oxford alligator print polished to a high gloss. But what was really impressive about Gary was his black curly hair that stood two inches high. Bill wondered if it was natural, or permed. Gary asked Don a question, and left. Don picked up a pipe from his desk, grabbed a pinch of tobacco with two fingers, then lightly tapped it down into the bowl with his right index finger.

"As I was saying, we offer training. Our business is selling foreign real estate. We are currently selling property on the island of Great Exuma for the Maguson Corporation, and housing and property at Horseshoe Bay, Texas for the Deltona Corporation. Horseshoe Bay has been featured twice on Lifestyles of the Rich and Famous. We will train you to pass an exam given by the Division of Securities in Columbus, Ohio. When you pass the exam, they will issue a license which we are required by law to display in the office. That license authorizes you to sell foreign real estate for Executive International Development Corporation." Don lit his pipe, then continued. "The Division of Securities defines foreign real estate as property outside of the state of Ohio. It's a six week training program, Executive International bears the cost for the exam, and Celeste schedules the appointment. You provide your own transportation to and from Columbus. Are you interested?" Don asked, puffing on his pipe. A mild smoke floated upwards and the aroma of walnuts filled the room.

"Of course!" Bill smiled.

"Be here at six o'clock, Our classes are held in the conference room down the hall and I am the instructor." Don grinned.

\* \* \*

Bill called his parole officer and reported that he had a job. He didn't seem to care, one way or another. His words were, "Make sure that you send in your monthly report."

Bonnie was a little more excited with the news. They talked for awhile, and Bill expressed his concern about his not having a better wardrobe. Bonnie said that she could help with that. She broke out her sewing machine and carefully measured Bill. She made shirts, a vest, and tried her hand at a three piece suit. Finished, she proudly presented the suit to Bill. It was an odd shade of green, a jean type material, and the lapel was much larger than most suits. It wasn't to Bill's liking, but he would never tell Bonnie that. She had worked hard and he truly appreciated her effort.

At training, Bill looked around the conference room. There were seven or eight trainees, all much older than himself. He guessed they were retirees looking for something to occupy their time or supplement their income. Whatever their reason, there was a common goal - passing the exam.

Six weeks later, Bill made the trip to Columbus. The traffic in the City was bumper to bumper, a stench filled the air, horns honked, and pedestrians scurried about on the concrete sidewalks. Some stood waiting for a light to turn red while others simply jaywalked. Baltimore was different, the hustle and bustle was neon signs, the night life of clubs and parties. Columbus reminded Bill of a colony of ants moving from one place to another as fast as they could. They were the workers, the people with office jobs who filled the highrise office buildings.

Bill drove into an underground parking garage stopping at a toll booth where he was handed a time stamped ticket. He asked for directions to the Security Exchange Building.

"To the right, one block down, across the street on the left." The attendant said. Bill repeated the directions to himself several times as he parked the van in the first available parking space. When he entered the building, he looked at the directory, the Division of Securities was on the ninth floor. Once inside the office, he was given a questionnaire to fill out. Name, address, date of birth, state he was born in, fathers name, mothers maiden name, and the name and address of the corporation sponsoring his application. The last question was, "Have you ever been convicted for a felony?" Check yes, or no. He checked neither, leaving both boxes blank. After completing the form, he was directed to a room where about thirty people were seated waiting to take the exam which consisted of a hundred questions with multiple choice answers. A box was next to each answer, check the correct one. Ninety minutes was allowed for the exam. One hour later, Bill raised his hand to get the examiner's attention.

"Yes sir." the examiner asked.

"If we're finished, can we leave?"

"Are you finished?"

"Yes, I am."

"Bring me your exam." After looking it over, he added. "You can leave. Your sponsor will be notified within two weeks of the results." he added.

# CHAPTER SEVEN
## GOOMBAY SMASH

Two weeks later, Don Conley called and asked Bill to stop by his office.

"I'll be there in thirty minutes!" Bill replied, wondering if there was a problem. His worst fear was his prior criminal history having been discovered. As he walked through the door Gary and Celeste said in unison, "Congratulations!" Gary had just finished hanging Bill's license on the wall along with his, Don Conley's, and the other representatives of Executive International Development Corporation.

Don stepped out of his office, congratulated Bill, and asked if he had a brief case.

"Of course!" Bill lied, he didn't own one.

"Out of twenty-eight people who took the exam, besides yourself, only one other person passed." Gary reported, smiling.

"Most people have to take the exam at least twice." Celeste added.

"Welcome to the madhouse," she giggled. Bill had noticed that Celeste was exceptionally nice. Always polite and courteous. On the phone, she had the voice of an angel. Through general conversations, he had learned that she was married with two small children, both boys. Celeste was in her early forties, pleasantly plump, and normally wore black or gray slacks, a white blouse with frills, and a jacket. And there was always fresh flowers on her desk.

"Would you like to go on an appointment with me this evening?" Don offered.

"Absolutely." Bill snapped.

"Let's meet at the office at six o' clock." Don suggested, grinning.

Leaving the office, Bill drove directly to the Parma Town Mall. At the May Company department store he purchased a gray Samsonite brief case. Then he rode the escalator upstairs where he filled out an application for a credit card. He stopped at a shoe store in the Mall and bought a pair of black dress shoes. His last stop was at Suits are Us. He purchased a shiny dark brown suit with a chocolate dark lace design that ran the full length of the trousers and around the lapel of the jacket. He wasn't sure if it was Italian, or Mexican because he had never seen anything like it before. The second suit he purchased was a gray pin-stripe. He purchased two dress shirts, two ties, and a gold colored tie clip to complete his attire.

Returning to the apartment he showered, shaved, and dressed. As he brought Lee up on the days events, he made a quick sandwich.

"I need your help tomorrow." Lee said.

"For what?"

"I bought a bed and a dresser for two hundred dollars from a guy that's moving out of Regency Towers tomorrow."

At six o'clock Bill pulled into the parking lot at the office. Don was waiting for him. He looked at Bill approvingly and they walked into the office.

"Open your brief case." Don instructed, filling it with brochures of the property in the Bahamas on Great Exuma, contracts, and a video of the island.

Gary was still in his office, his silver 1979 Cadillac El Dorado was parked next to Don's 1980 metallic brown Cadillac Coupe Deville.

Fifteen minutes later they left the office in Don's Cadillac. It had every luxury feature available and still had that new car smell.

"The property in Texas, Horseshoe Bay, was featured twice on Lifestyles of the Rich and Famous. It has two Robert Trent golf courses, two marinas, shopping centers, five star restaurants, and a private airport. If you want, you can park your airplane next to your house. The security drives black Rolls Royces, and the cheapest condo starts at a quarter of a million dollars."

"That's impressive."

"The appointment tonight is for property in the Bahamas. Those lots start at ten thousand dollars and the commission paid is seven percent. For instance, if you sell a ten thousand piece of property, the commission is seven hundred dollars."

The perspective buyers home was a white split level in a modest neighborhood. Two vehicles were parked in an asphalt driveway, a white Chevrolet Blazer with oversize tires and a newer red foreign compact that was either a Honda, or Datsun.

Don Conley introduced Bill as a new representative who was there to observe. The husband and wife were fine with that.

He began by asking the couple to fill out a questionnaire while he set a projector up. The questionnaire was basic name, address, place of employment, phone number, names and ages of children. The purpose of the questionnaire was to introduce the ink pen to the client and make them feel comfortable having it in their hand. In conversation, Bill learned the couple were newlyweds, married less than a year. The wife was a school teacher at Brecksville High School and the husband was a factory worker at Caterpillar. They both had brown hair, enjoyed running marathons, were of average height and weight, and appeared to be in excellent physical condition.

Don gave a speech using a ton of adjectives to describe the island of Great Exuma. It was beautiful, gorgeous, with breathtaking views and spectacular sunsets. It was "an unspoiled island".

"Do you mind if I smoke?" Don asked, taking his pipe from his pocket and holding it up.

The wife handed him an ash tray.

Don removed his jacket, hanging it on the back of the chair. He grabbed a pouch of tobacco and filled the pipe, a ritual he performed many times throughout the day. Then he adjusted the slide screen projector focusing it on a white wall. He cuffed his sleeves exposing his gold watch and bracelet, asked the husband to turn off the kitchen light, and turned the projector on. The slides of the island were beautifully narrated and set to music. The island was exciting, romantic, and captivating. It was magnificent!

Don concluded the presentation by explaining to the young couple that he wasn't going to ask them to make a decision today to purchase the property. Instead, he proposed the couple decide today to go to the island and inspect the property themselves. He explained. "I will write a contract for a specific piece of property and you give me a check for One thousand dollars. That money will be placed in an escrow account. It's just earnest money! Executive International Development Corporation will pay 'all expenses' to send the two of you to the island for three days and two nights. We will pay for your airfare, motel, and meals. A representative will meet you at the airport and show you around the island. Before you leave, you will be asked to make one of three decisions. One, buy the property. Two, perhaps you would like to switch your property for another lot. An ocean front, a hilltop, or a lot adjacent to the airport. That's your option. Three, you can say it's nice, but it's not for you. In that event, we ask that you pay one-half of the airfare. The only requirement of Executive International Development Corporation is that you visit the property within 90-days."

The couple agreed to the terms.

Don stopped at a Holiday Inn to celebrate the sale with cocktails. The Holiday and Harley Inns were near the office on Snow Road across the street from each other and they both had nice bars.

"I make more money selling the property at Horseshoe Bay because that includes housing, but the property in the Bahamas pretty much sells itself and you get the commission faster. Within 90-days! With housing you get paid when the contract is written, when ground is broke, and at closing."

"How do you get the appointments?"

"Executive provides us with brochures and cardboard stands. You will need to have a rubber stamp made with your name and phone number on it. Stamp the back of the brochures, then place those in restaurants, supermarkets, beauty salons wherever you think someone may pick one up and read it. If they call the office for you, Celeste will take their name and phone number or set-up an appointment. Gary rents a booth at the Convention Center for the Sportsman's Show and other events. But the majority of your leads will come by word of mouth - referrals."

Returning to the apartment Bill called Bonnie, then Jerry. Bill was excited. In his heart he knew that he could prepare a better presentation than Don Conley.

\* \* \*

Lee and Bobby Hardin were sitting at the bar laughing when Bill entered the Ground Round. Lee grinned, and Bobby told the barmaid to give Bill a drink.

"Seven and Seven, Sandy." Bill smiled, turning his attention to Bobby. "You should see the property that I'm selling in the Bahamas. It's on an unspoiled island, Great Exuma."

"It's probably underwater in the winter." Lee chuckled.

He twirled the ice in his glass, then took a sip.

"It's probably better known as Seagull shit island." Bobby chimed in, laughing.

"Go ahead, make your jokes." Bill frowned.

"Have you been there, Billy?" Bobby asked.

"You know I haven't!"

"When you can tell me that you've been there yourself, then I will be more inclined to listen to whatever you have to say." Bobby concluded.

Back at the apartment, Bill thought about what Bobby had said and he wanted to visit the island himself. There was only one thing preventing him from doing that - money.

Bill still hadn't gone to the DMV to buy Ohio tags for the van. Sandy had told him the easiest way was through Triple-A. She had explained there were a lot of advantages to becoming a member. So, Bill joined. He was given a booklet listing all of their services. He purchased the Ohio license tags, then insured the van with Allstate. After reading through the booklet, he applied for a Passport. For an additional seven dollars and fifty-cents he purchased an International Driver's license.

The training sessions were completed. But on Thursday afternoon Bill was still required to attend the sales meeting. At the sales meeting, Bill presented Don Conley with a contract and a thousand dollar check. Bill's first sale was to himself. Celeste made the arrangements for the flight, motel, and meals. Hearing what Bill had done, Gary walked into the meeting to congratulate him. He told the other sales representatives they could learn a lesson from this. It was important, at least to Bill, for him to be able to say that he had purchased property on the island. He was investing One thousand dollars, but his commission would reimburse Seven hundred of that. If for some reason he didn't like the property, he could cancel and simply pay for half of the airfare. It just made good sense, he thought.

Later that night, Bill called Bonnie and asked. "Would you like to take a trip with me?"

"Where to?"

"The Bahamas."

"Don't tease me!"

"I'm serious. Do you want to go, or not?"

"Of course I do!" Bonnie felt like the Queen of the ball.

Bill smiled, knowing that she was a happy girl.

Celeste made the reservations two weeks in advance. From Cleveland they would fly American Airlines to Miami International. In Miami, they could fly on a twin engine turbo prop to the island of Great Exuma. Vernon Curtis, a representative for the Magnusan Corporation would meet them at the airport and drive them to their motel, the Peace and Plenty. Vernon would be their host and show them around the island.

It was miserably hot when the airplane landed at Miami International. The airport was huge with crowds of people scurrying from one place to another. They picked up their luggage from the baggage area on the lower level, then asked a flight attendant for directions. Once outside, through the blinding sunlight they saw their airplane, and boarded. There were twenty seats, less than half filled. Bill graciously allowed Bonnie the window. The humidity was horrid, and they were anxious to get airborne knowing that would cool them.

Great Exuma was one hundred and ten miles northwest of Miami, a forty-five minute flight. As the airplane lifted off, Bonnie marveled at the beaches of Miami. Palm trees lined the city streets. On the beach, sunbathers spread colorful blankets. There were swimmers in the water, surfers, and people playing volleyball. Twenty minutes into the flight, looking out the window, Bonnie saw small islands with bare strips of land and barrels on both sides. Wrecked boats and small airplanes were visible in the water.

"I hope our airplane doesn't meet that fate!" Bonnie sighed, feeling uneasy.

There were two other couples on the airplane. The guys were tanned and wore expensive watches and thick gold chains around their necks. They wore shorts, colorful Hawaiian shirts, and sandals. The girls were young, beautiful, and obviously spoiled.

The airplane landed on a dirt runway, not large enough to accommodate Commercial Airliners. At the far end of the runway, there was a yellow Bulldozer. It was a very windy day. Small aircraft lined up, waiting their turn to taxi down the runway and take-off.

As they disembarked, before them was a small concrete building, a sign read: CUSTOMS. Inside, there was a long folding table and two black officers. They were dressed in green shorts, green short sleeve shirts, and wore green hats with black paten leather half -moon brims. In the center of the hat was a gold badge.

A Customs officer asked Bill to put their luggage on top of the table, opening each suitcase he browsed through it, and asked how long they intended to stay. He closed the suitcases, sending them on their way. They were in one door and out the other in a matter of minutes.

As they stepped outside, there was an old white windowed van with a very short black man leaning against it wearing white shorts, a colorful Hawaiian short sleeve shirt with only the bottom two buttons buttoned, and dusty brown sandals.

"Hi! Welcome to Great Exuma. You picked a fine time to visit." Vernon Curtis laughed.

"Why's that?" Bill asked.

"Aw, you don't know. My man, there's a hurricane coming. That's why all of the small airplanes are flying inland!"

"A hurricane?" Bonnie repeated, looking very afraid.

"Hurricane Fredrick." Vernon grinned, his teeth noticeably white.

Bill introduced himself, then Bonnie. The trio stopped at a grass shack directly across from Customs. A sign above the entrance read: KERMIT'S.

"This is my partner's bar." Vernon laughed, adding. "He might not have it after tonight."

Kermit's was a grass shack with a bar, padded stools, and a very friendly bartender named Kermit. He and Vernon owned the boat that took the mail back and forth to Miami. Both men spoke with thick British accents. They were Bohemians. Veron explained that Lord Rholes deeded sixty-percent of the Bahamas to the Bohemians. It's generation land, and it can never be sold. It can be leased, the other forty-percent can be sold.

The airport was a dirt runway, There was only one dirt road to town and it was filled with potholes.

"Unspoiled island, huh?" Bill chuckled.

The Peace and Plenty was painted aqua blue. It had a restaurant and separate bar. Their room had a double bed, a bathroom with a shower, and double doors that opened to a small balcony that overlooked a cove. The ocean splashed against the retaining wall beneath them. Sailboats were moored in the cove seeking shelter from the hurricane. There was no TV in the room, and no phone. When Vernon dropped them off, he promised to return in the morning.

Bill and Bonnie showered, dressed, and went to the restaurant for dinner. Their waitress informed them there was only one phone, and it was at the desk in the Main lobby. In the morning, there was a newspaper in the lobby for guest to read. As they waited for dinner, they learned the Bohemians had three speeds. Slow, slower, and slowest.

When the winds picked-up, the lights went out, and the residents of the motel sought refuge in the bar. There were also those who abandoned their sailboats. Bill pointed out to Bonnie that one of the females had more hair on her legs than he did.

"Be nice!" Bonnie giggled.

There was a skull with crossbones hanging on a wall above a black kettle. The sign at the top of it read GOOMBAY SMASH which peeked Bonnie's curiosity. She asked. "What's that?"

"It's an island drink made of many Rums," the bartender explained. "And it's a very potent concoction."

Bill and Bonnie ordered Goombay smashes. The drink was sweet with no taste of alcohol though the coconut Rum was 100 proof.

Against the back wall was a shelf with a short wave radio, tuned in.

It reported the eye of the hurricane was directly over Great Exuma. There was a quietness, an aerie silence, and then the wind picked up tossing the sailboats wildly.

They returned to their motel room tired, inebriated, and quickly fell asleep. The next morning Bill awoke to a loud pounding on the door and Vernon yelling. "Wake-up! Let's go for a ride, my friend."

Bonnie stayed in bed. Bill's head was throbbing, but he dressed and went to tour the island with Vernon to survey the damage. Palm trees were laying in the road. A house on a hilltop had lost its roof. Kermit's bar had survived the night, and there was no report of injuries.

The town of Georgetown was on Great Exuma, and it was the Capital of the Bahamas. Vernon Curtis was Governor Pinling's nephew.

Vernon never once called Bill by his name, he always referred to him as "my friend".

After breakfast, Bill and Bonnie walked through Georgetown. All of the buildings were pink, including City Hall. Store owners were busily removing plywood from the boarded up windows of their shops, while others picked-up fallen palm tree branches and swept sidewalks. Bill and Bonnie strolled off and down a white sandy beach, hand in hand.

Later that night, they drank and danced to the beat of Congo drums beneath a thatched straw roof hut. It was across the street from the motel, and an atmosphere like none other they had experienced.

After spending two days on the island, Bill found a deep appreciation for it. Its natural beauty was unmatched! The owner of the Peace and Plenty previously owned a machine shop in Akron, Ohio. After two heart attacks, he sold everything and moved to the island. Bill thought that someday, he may retire there too!

The lot Bill purchased through Executive International Development Corporation cost ten thousand dollars. Before he left the island, Vernon sold "his friend" an ocean front lot, a hilltop lot, and a lot adjacent to the airport for ten thousand dollars - no down payment required. Bill also opened a numbered checking and savings account.

# CHAPTER EIGHT
## EXECUTIVE'S CLUB

Returning to Cleveland Bill dropped Bonnie off at her house, then stopped by the office.

"I swear, Bill. I didn't know about the hurricane when I made the reservations. You were boarding the airplane in Miami when I first found out about it." Celeste announced as he walked into the office.

Bill smiled, and replied. "The first clue that we had was when we flew onto the island, all of the smaller aircraft were lined-up to fly to the mainland. The second clue was as we drove to the motel, store owners were outside boarding up windows. It was quite an experience.

Don and Gary both stepped out of their offices, smiling, anxious to hear Bill's story.

"When Vernon Curtis picked us up at the airport and said that we could've picked a better time, my gut was telling me that something was terribly wrong. My girlfriend Bonnie and I spent the night at the bar at the Peace and Plenty drinking Goombay smashes and listening to weather reports on a short wave radio. Sailboats moored in the cove, the electric went out, and when the eye of hurricane Fredrick passed over the island there was a aerie calm. Then the winds picked up and blew for another two hours. The next morning, Vernon picked me up and we rode around the island surveying the damage. A house on a hilltop lost its roof. There were fallen palm trees and leaves spread about, but there were no reported injuries.

Don grinned, and lit his pipe.

Bill looked at him, and said. "Now I understand why you refer to Great Exuma as an unspoiled island."

Gary turned, laughed, and walked back to his office.

"The airport is under construction. It has been under construction for the past ten years. But City Hall has voted to issue a gambling license which is going to bring a casino to the island. That's huge!" Don chuckled.

"To be completely truthful. At first, I hated the island. The pot holes, no paved roads, no TV, no phone. I felt like a castaway on Gilligan's island. Not to mention the Bohemians have three speeds. Slow, slower, and slowest. Two days later I was in love with the white sandy beaches, crystal blue water, and the warm trade winds, and the tranquility. I didn't want to leave!"

Celeste smiled.

"The island would be better off left unspoiled," Bill thoughtfully added.

* * *

Returning to his apartment, Bill stopped at his mailbox. There was some junk mail along with a credit card from the May Company. The credit card only had a two hundred dollar balance, but that was fine. He now had a loan, a checking and savings account, a Visa and Mastercard, and a May Company department store card.

Later that day, Bill picked up applications for gas credit cards. Shell, American, and Standard Oil.

Jerry called to inform Bill that Richard Biggerstaff had called from Oklahoma, promising to be in Dayton within the next thirty days. Bill shared in Jerry's excitement. "That's fantastic! Bonnie and I just returned from a trip to the Bahamas. I purchased some properties, and while I was there I opened a numbered checking and savings account."

Jerry reminded Bill to keep his eye on one thing - Octopool! the following week. Bill passed out brochures in restaurants, beauty salons, and a bowling alley. He walked through the Parma Mall in search of places to set-up racks of brochures. He stopped at a barber shop, sat down in a chair, and waited to get a haircut. From a magazine rack, he picked up a U.S.A. Today and browsed through it. An article caught his eye. Property in the sunshine states appreciate ten percent a year. It occurred to Bill that property in the Bahamas should be marketed as "investment opportunity."

While sitting in the barber chair, he pondered the thought, told the barber about his recent trip to the unspoiled island and said that it was a great investment opportunity. The barber listened intently, and Bill offered to set-up an appointment to show him a slide presentation. The barber gave Bill his name, phone number, and scheduled an appointment for the following Monday night.

Later that evening, at the Ground Round, Bill told Bobby Hardin about his trip to the Bahamas, hurricane Fredrick, and what a great investment opportunity it was. Bobby scheduled an appointment for the following Tuesday night.

The next day, Bill stopped in the Dollar Bank offering to buy Vaughn Medcalf lunch. Vaughn was too busy to take him up on the offer and asked for a rain check. Before leaving, Bill told Vaughn about his trip, hurricane Fredrick, and the great investment opportunity.

"I have an appointment Tuesday night to show Bobby a slide presentation, do you think you could join us?"

"I promise that I will do my best to make it."

Thursday, before the sales meeting, Bill handed Celeste three contracts with thousand dollar checks. "Bobby Hardin and Vaughn Medcalf would like to be scheduled to go together. They would like separate rooms, but only two airline tickets will be required."

After the sales meeting, Gary asked to see Bill in his office.

"Close the door behind you." Gary instructed.

To Bill's right was a small conference table and chairs. To his left, Gary's dark Mahogany desk which was much larger than most. Bill's first thought was the Division of Securities had called exposing his past felony convictions.

Directly in front of Gary's desk were two soft brown leather chairs. Against another wall was a matching brown leather couch, and a bar with two stools. There was a small refrigerator, potted trees, and hanging plants. On another wall hung an assortment of diplomas. Behind Gary's huge high back brown leather chair was a row of curtained windows that ran from the floor to the ceiling and wall to wall. Gary motioned for Bill to have a seat, as he sat behind his desk. Gary congratulated Bill on his sales. Then, he asked. "Would you be interested in assuming the lease on my 1979 El Dorado? I want to lease a new Lincoln Towncar, but in order for me to do that I need someone assume the lease on the El Dorado. There's twelve monthly payments of three hundred and seventy-five dollars."

They walked outside to look at the El Dorado. The seats were silver leather with Cadillac Emblems stitched into the back of each seat. "I had the electric sunroof installed by Roman's Chariot." Gary proudly declared. The dash was wood grain. The El Dorado had power seats, windows, and mirrors. It was equipped with climate control air-conditioning, cruise control, tilt wheel, and a stereo sound system. The silver metallic paint was set off by wire wheels. And, there was less than ten thousand miles on the odometer.

"I would love to have the El Dorado, but I'm not sure that my credit is good enough."

Gary and Bill returned to the office. Bill changed the subject by asking Gary what he thought about selling the property in the Bahamas as "investment opportunity".

Gary was impressed with the concept. He told Bill that he spends the majority of his time putting syndications together, then asked Bill if he knew what that was?

"No!" Bill replied honestly.

"I find a project. For instance, a builder may need money to build fifty condos and he isn't willing to assume all of the risk. I may purchase ten of those condos before they are built at a reduced price. I form a syndication, which is bringing together a group of investors. I become an equal partner and receive a share of the profit after the condo's are built, and sold. It's a win-win situation for everyone. If there's no profit, then I don't make a dime. But I always make money." Gary said, with a smile.

"Have you ever thought about holding Seminars?" Bill asked. "I have done that, and I wouldn't be opposed to trying it again if you have a better presentation. Back to the El Dorado. There is only one year left on the lease. If necessary, I will co-sign for you."

Bill cheerfully agreed to assume the lease. The following day he met Gary at the Cadillac dealership on Pearl Road in Parma Heights and Gary co-signed for Bill to assume the lease.

Bill drove straight to Bonnie's house, pulled into the driveway, and honked the horn. Bonnie looked out the kitchen window, saw Bill getting out of the El Dorado, and shot out the door. She wrapped her arms around his neck and kissed him. As a second thought, she asked. "Whose car is that?"

"It's mine." Bill grinned.

"No, it's not!" Bonnie snapped, then asked. "Is it?"

"Yes, it is. I just assumed the lease from Gary Archdeacon. He leased a new Lincoln Towncar. Want to go for a ride?"

Bonnie ran into the house, grabbed her purse, and she was back in a flash.

"Let's go shopping. The May Company sent me a credit card with a two hundred dollar limit."

At the May Company Bill purchased a gold pen and pencil set, two pair of dress slacks, two Polo shirts, and a pair of soft brown leather loafers.

In another store, Bill fell in love with a bar. It was a light brown wood grain two piece bar. Each section was six feet long. A soft thick tan leather cushion ran around the edge of the bar. A chrome footrest ran across the bottom, and it came with four matching stools. The bar was on sale, marked down from eighteen hundred dollars to seven hundred dollars. Knowing how much Bill liked the bar, Bonnie charged it to her Visa. When the bar was delivered, Bill placed it in the living room. He built a shelf with mirrors behind the bar and stocked it with bourbons, whiskey, vodka, and Scotch.

The next day, Bill stopped at the printing shop and ordered business cards, gloss black with gold print. Executive International Development Corporation, 1440 Snow Road, Parma, Ohio was centered. In the bottom left corner was BILL BURNS, SALES REPRESENTATIVE with the business and his home phone number. Returning to the apartment, he stopped to check the mailbox. Inside an envelope, he discovered a Passport! Inside the apartment, Bill opened the gray Samsonite briefcase, clipped the matching gold pen and pencil set to the divider, then inserted his Passport and International Driver's license into a pocket, so that it would be seen whenever he opened his briefcase.

Then, he joined the ranks of the elite, he became a member of the Sales and Marketing Executives Club of Greater Cleveland. As a member, he received a wooden plaque with his name engraved in gold.

## CHAPTER NINE
## THE BIG DAY

It was eight o'clock in the morning. Bill had showered, shaved, dressed, and was cooking breakfast when the phone rang.

"Hello?"

"Richard will be here Saturday afternoon. You're going to be here to meet him, aren't you?" Jerry asked.

"Of course! By the way, I joined Triple-A, applied for a Passport, and I received it in the mail yesterday."

"Nothing with you surprises me," Jerry countered, with a chuckle.

After hanging up from Jerry, Bill called Bonnie. "Would you like to go to Dayton this weekend. We could leave Saturday morning and stay at the Comfort Inn overnight." Bill had talked about Octopool often enough, and she shared in his excitement. She knew that Sunday was "the big day".

Saturday afternoon when Bill pulled in front of Jerry's apartment, he honked the horn. Jerry looked out the window, opened the sliding glass door, and stepped onto the patio. Seeing the silver El Dorado, he yelled. "I'll be right down!"

Jerry walked around the car with an approving eye, saying. "Nice, very nice." He opened the driver's door, sat down in the silver leather seat, ran his hand over the velvet headliner, then grabbed a handle and slid the panel back exposing the tinted sunroof. With the press of a button, the sunroof retracted.

"Auto Theft is a serious crime?" Jerry taunted.

"It's leased." Bill grinned.

"What did that set you back?"

"Three hundred and seventy-five dollars a month for the next twelve months, so we better start making money soon."

As they walked into the apartment Lynn was in the kitchen preparing a roast. Bill looked towards the corner, and said. "Hello Ralph."

Bonnie walked into the kitchen and asked Lynn if she needed any help.

"Want a drink?" Jerry offered.

"Seven and Seven." Bill replied. When Jerry looked in the girl's direction, they both shook their heads no.

Jerry made Bill a drink, and himself a Jack Daniel's and Coca-Cola on ice.

"How about a game of backgammon." Jerry suggested, as they settled on the couch in the living room. Jerry placed the game on the coffee table, and they argued intensely about who was going to be white, then who was going to roll first.

"Stop arguing!" Lynn screamed. "I swear, they're worse than a couple of two years old," she told Bonnie.

Bill suggested that Jerry put a white chip in one hand and a brown in the other. If Bill picked the white chip, then he would be white and roll first.

"It was my idea to play the game, so I should be the one choosing," Jerry argued.

"Boys will be boys!" Bonnie giggled.

At five o'clock, Richard called. He was at a Seventy-Six gas station, which was directly across the street from the Comfort Inn where Bill and Bonnie had reservations. Richard was less than ten minutes away from the apartment. Jerry gave directions, and five minutes later he and Bill stepped onto the balcony with drinks in hand to await his arrival. They leaned against a black wrought iron railing waiting for Richard to drive into the parking lot. Jerry hadn't thought to ask what kind of vehicle Richard was driving. The last time they had seen Richard was in federal prison. They were all wearing khaki pants and shirts with black laced shoes. Richard was the tallest among them standing six feet two. He weighed two hundred pounds. His blonde hair, when combed gave the appearance of a Harvard graduate. And his blue eyes were his best feature. Richard had a habit of brushing his hair to the right with his hand to get it out of his face. His blonde hair and big nose came from his Swedish ancestry. His high pitch baritone voice was clear, precise, and decisive. But it was his knowledge of corporate structure, financing, and accounting that impressed Bill, and Jerry. Most importantly, Richard claimed to have the connections needed to obtain the financing for Octopool. Having that, Jerry and Bill were willing to make Richard an equal partner.

An old yellow Ford truck, rusting around the rear fender wells creeped slowly into the parking lot. Inside the cab were three occupants - a man, woman, and a young child. The male driver was looking up at the apartments. Seeing Bill and Jerry, Richard stuck his hand out the window and waved. They could see him grinning through the windshield. He parked facing the building, shut the engine off, and it sputtered as if that was its dying breath. Richard was wearing blue jeans, a white short sleeve shirt open at the collar, and the prison issued black laced shoes.

Jerry welcomed him with a firm handshake, a hug, and a pat on the back. Bill shook his hand. Richard introduced his female companion as his girlfriend and the three year old girl as his daughter. The little girl had blonde hair, blue eyes, and was immediately drawn to Bill. Inside the apartment, she sat on his lap, asked one question after another, and wanted to play with his rose colored glasses.

Jerry made drinks, while Lynn announced that she had made a pot roast with potatoes and carrots. "I hope you haven't eaten?" Lynn asked.

"We're starved! We drove straight through, stopping for gas and restroom breaks. The truck wasn't all that bad on gas, and it only used four quarts of oil."

After dinner, the men excused themselves to talk business. "I made a prototype of Octopool!" Jerry said, proudly.

"That's great! But things haven't gone quite the way I planned. All of my connections were either deceased or had moved away when I was released. But to be true to my word, I'm here to help with whatever I can."

Bonnie asked Lynn if she knew that Richard was bringing his girlfriend and her daughter.

"It was a surprise to me." Lynn sighed.

Jerry and Bill were beside themselves - speechless. Jerry forced a smile, and told Richard there would be better days.

Bill had his doubts about that. He said his goodbyes, telling Jerry that he would give him a call later in the week.

"Well, that was disappointing." Bill told Bonnie, as they drove out of the parking lot.

Bill and Bonnie checked into the Comfort Inn.

"Did Jerry know that Richard wasn't coming by himself?" Bonnie asked Bill.

"I don't know."

"I don't think he knew. Lynn didn't know anything about it.

The next morning, the drive back to Cleveland seemed to be much longer. He thought of Jerry telling him "to keep his eye on the ball - Octopool." He wondered what Jerry was thinking now.

Bill dropped Bonnie off at her house kissing her with a promise to call later that night. Returning to Regency Towers, he parked the Eldorado next to the customized Dodge van in the rear parking lot.

Lee was sitting at the dining room table. Behind him, the wall had been wallpapered with an Autumn scene.

"Nice job!" Bill said, admiring the scenery, it was mostly browns and golds.

That night Bill called Bonnie and they talked for about two hours.

* * *

It was two weeks before Bill called Jerry. Richard and his family were still there. Richard was in the process of going into business for himself. The law in Ohio required every in-ground swimming pool to have a fence around it. Jerry was selling swimming pools. Richard already had a truck. Jerry financed the business. He loaned Richard the money to purchase tools, fencing, and materials.

Bill couldn't help but ask. "Did you know that Richard was bringing his family?"

"No! But I'm hoping he makes enough money to pay me back and rent a place of his own. Lynn is really upset with their living with us."

"I'm wondering if he ever had any connections, When people move, they generally leave a forwarding address."

Jerry was at a loss of what to say.

By the end of the month, Bill closed three more deals.

# CHAPTER TEN
# EASY MON£Y

At the sales meeting Thursday night, Gary made an announcement. "There's going to be a wine and cheese party at the Harley Inn next Friday night at seven o' clock. Each of you will be given tables for two couples. Please give the names of your potential clients to Celeste no later than Thursday morning. Bill Burns will be in-charge of this seminar, if you have any questions."

The next day Bill returned to the barber shop in the Parma Mall hoping the U.S.A. Today magazine would still be on the rack of magazines. In hindsight, he wished that he had made a mental note of the date and issue. Good fortune smiled upon him, the magazine was still there and his barber cheerfully allowed him to take the magazine. Using a red ink pen, Bill drew circles around the pertinent information. Then, he spent the next few days perfecting his sales pitch.

Friday night, Bill arrived at the Harley Inn two hours early parking the El Dorado at the curb at the front entrance. He walked through the foyer and up to the front desk, wearing his fancy brown suit. The desk clerk pointed Bill in the direction of the reserved room. He found everything set-up and the caterers planned to serve the wine in plastic cups. Bill insisted they serve the wine in glasses and offer refills at the table. The caterer planned to serve everything else buffet style, selfserve. Bill insisted that platters of cheese and crackers be placed on tables with cardboard plaques that read "RESERVED FOR" with the last name of the couple for each table. Twelve tables were set-up with a yellow writing pad and an ink pen.

"I'm not a waiter!" the caterer complained.

"You are tonight. Or, you can pack it up, and leave. I have no problem ordering from the bar and restaurant."

The caterer walked away in a huff. Bill set-up the slide projector, dimmed the lights, and made sure that everything was working properly. Then, he walked to the front desk and requested a chalk board.

When Gary arrived, he parked his new metallic brown Lincoln Towncar behind Bill's El Dorado. And Don Conley parked his metallic brown Cadillac Coupe Deville behind Gary's Lincoln.

As the couple arrived, the sales representatives escorted their perspective buyers to their assigned tables. Bill introduced himself to each couple explaining their was pen and paper so they could make a note of any questions they may think of during the presentation. The pen and paper was theirs to keep!

"How do you want to do this?" Don Conley asked Bill.

"You open. I'll close."

Don opened with his speech describing the natural beauty of the island of Great Exuma." It's an unspoiled island!"

Bill chuckled, more to himself.

Gary dimmed the lights. Don started the slide projector. As the slides rolled, Bill watched the couples hoping to get a glimpse of which ones appeared to be more interested.

When the lights came on, Bill took center stage. "I have been to the island and purchased property myself. As a matter of fact when I flew in, all of the small aircraft flew inland. Nobody told me that hurricane Fredrick was on its way!"

Everyone shared a laugh.

"I can tell you that it has white sandy beaches, crystal blue water, and breathtaking views. It's a great place to retire. But, keep in mind that you don't have to retire there. Think of it as "an investment opportunity". U.S.A. Today reports that property in the sunshine states appreciates ten percent a year." Bill held the magazine high in the air for everyone to see. He pulled the chalkboard to the center of the room. On one side, he wrote One thousand dollars. On the other, he wrote ten thousand dollars. "The One thousand dollars represents your down payment. If you left that money in the bank with an annual interest of six percent, you would have a net profit of sixty dollars." Bill wrote the number sixty on the chalk board and circled it. "But if you put your One thousand dollars down on a ten thousand dollar piece of property and it appreciated at ten percent a year." Bill did the math on the chalkboard. "You're return on your investment is One thousand dollars. There's not a better or safer investment folks! I'm not asking that you purchase anything today. On behalf of Executive International Development Corporation I am authorized to present you with an opportunity. For those of you interested in hearing more, please remain seated. For those of you not interested, I thank you for your time and you are free to leave."

\* \* \*

Bobby and Vaughn returned from their trip to Great Exuma. Bobby purchased a second lot while he was there. The commission on the additional property would be split with Vernon Curtis, which was fine with Bill. He thought of it as a bonus because he did nothing to earn it.

Bobby was seated in his usual place at the Ground Round when Bill arrived.

"I'm going to need your help moving this weekend."

"Whose moving?" Bill asked.

"I am!" Bobby laughed. "I bought a two bedroom condo in Medina with my accountant."

"Are you serious? Where is Medina?"

"It's about twenty minutes away, if you take the expressway. Or, you can take State Road to Granger Road. Turn left on Granger, and it's a half mile down on the left. When you see the tennis courts, look to the right and my condo sits on top of the hill."

"Whenever you need me, I'll be available." Bill promised.

"Seven and Seven?" Sandy asked.

"Yes, darlin, thank you." Bill grinned.

If Sandy minded Bill calling her darlin, she didn't say so. It had long been established she didn't like anyone calling her sweetheart. Bill always thought to leave Sandy a generous tip.

\* \* \*

On the trip to Dayton, Bonnie was very talkative. "What is your birthday?" She asked.

"I was born December 3, 1947."

"Where?"

"In Lakeland, Florida."

"Is that where you grew up?"

"Not exactly. I spent my adulthood in Baltimore, Maryland. My parents moved to Maryland when I was seven years old. They divorced when I was twelve. My older brother and younger sister chose to stay with my mother. I had witnessed my mother's infidelity, so I chose to live with my father. He and I returned to Florida, and we lived in a motel for a year. To earn extra money I polished shoes in a barbershop, sold magazines door to door, and worked odd jobs. My father remarried when I was fourteen. I had two step sisters who were A and B students. My grades were barely passing. My stepmother and I never saw things eye to eye. I quit school when I was fifteen and moved out on my own. By the time I was sixteen I was married. I have two daughters, Tina Marie and Kerri Ann. I was a terrible husband. We were both too young for that responsibility. Not to mention that I cheated on my wife. She divorced me! I made five trips to Florida in search of my wife and the kids. I found her remarried, and my daughters were calling her husband daddy. They didn't know who I was!"

"Do - "

"Hey! I feel like I'm being interrogated!"

Bonnie smiled, then said. "You're thirty-three."

They arrived at Jerry's apartment at one o'clock. Jerry quickly announced that he and Bill were going for a ride, they had some business to discuss.

"Give me the keys." Jerry said, on their way down the steps to the parking lot, anxious to drive the El Dorado. Jerry opened the driver's door, sat down, then flipped the switch to unlock the passenger door. "I could get use to this," He smiled

"No, you can't!" Bill grinned.

A few minutes later Jerry parked in front of a store in a small strip Mall.

The sign above the door read CENTURY ENTERTAINMENT in black and gold lettering.

"I just want you to take a look at this." Jerry grinned. Once inside, he introduced Bill to the business partners, Ken and Jim. The store was small, but nice. The floor was carpeted. Behind a counter was a display filled with film and flash bulbs. Colorful posters decorated the walls, and there was an abundance of Kodak memorabilia. A tall rack displayed leather-like carrying cases. In the rear of the store, there were three rooms.

"This is my brother, Bill." Jerry announced.

"Pleased to meet you." Ken smiled, extending his hand in friendship." Jerry has told us quite a lot about you."

"Anything good?" Bill grinned.

"All good!" Ken said assuringly. "We are going to be opening new stores throughout Ohio in the near future. If your half as good as your brother claims, we would love to invite you to join our sales team."

"What exactly is it that you sell?"

"We sell the developing of film. Our secretary mails out cards to perspective buyers offering a brand new Bell and Howell movie camera and projector FREE, if they agree to do their film processing with us."

"How is that profitable?"

"At the conclusion of the presentation, we obligate the customer to develop three hundred rolls of film with us. They have a lifetime in which to do that, and they can purchase their film anywhere."

"What's the catch?" Bill asked flatly, thinking that if something is too good to be true, it generally is.

"The customer prepays their processing in one of three ways. Cash, Visa, or our convenient payment plan which is financed."

"Let me show you my office." Jerry insisted.

His office consisted of a folding card table, three folding chairs, and a shelf that displayed a Bell and Howell Super 8 movie camera and projector. On the table was a scrap book with pictures of for instances that someone might use the camera for. Birthdays, Christmas, weddings, picnics, football games, family events.

Bill wasn't impressed, or interested. He still felt that Jerry would be far better off to join him at Executive International Development Corporation.

Leaving the store, they stopped at Best Products. Jerry wanted to price a new video player. Bill browsed through the jewelry department. The clerk said that with proper identification he would accept a personal check. So, Bill bought matching gold chains for him, and Jerry. And matching gold rings with two diamonds and a Ruby for Bonnie, and Lynn. Jerry said that he would later surprise Bill with something unique to put on the chains.

Bonnie and Lynn were pleasantly surprised, promising the guys could leave for a couple of hours anytime as long as they returned with gifts.

* * *

At Thursday night's sales meeting, Gary made an announcement. "Executive International is undertaking a major project with tremendous potential for everyone involved. In Florida, we are going to be selling property and housing in nine resort communities for the Deltona Corporation." Gary smiled, looked at Bill and said. "And Bill Burns is being promoted to Sales Manager. All sales representatives will be reporting directly to him. Don will handle the property at Horsehoe Bay exclusively. I will give everyone an update at next weeks sales meeting."

Gary walked Bill from the conference back to the office. "And this will be your office," Gary grinned, opening the office door directly across from Don Conley's.

Bill glanced around the room. There was a desk, three chairs, and boxes piled in a corner. Nothing impressive!

"Pack your bags." Gary announced. "I know it's short notice, but we've got an eight o' clock flight to catch. I'll meet you at the airport."

Bill looked at his cheap Timex watch. It was four o' clock.

He rushed home, packed, told Lee that he was going out of town on business and that he would be back in a few days. At the airport, Gary explained that everything was happening fast, that he was just given the property yesterday by the Deltona Corporation.

"The purpose of the trip is to inspect and familiarize ourselves with all nine resort properties, then visit Deltona's Headquarters in Miami!'

They flew into Naples, Florida. From there, it was a twenty minute ride to Marco Island, the condos were luxurious with ocean views.

The following morning Bill called Bonnie to let her know that he wouldn't be seeing her that weekend.

"Why? Is there a problem?" Bonnie wanted to know.

"Yes. I'm in Florida with Gary Archdeacon on a business trip."

"Call me when you get back!" Bonnie laughed.

Gary and Bill flew to Saint Augustine to join a tour bus filled with representatives from other states. The tour began with Saint Augustine Shores where property and housing was being sold. Some of the nine communities across Florida were less expensive than others, but all of the housing was new construction.

In Miami, Bill stood before Deltona Corporations towering building. The facade of the building was blue with dark tinted windows. It was on a two lane street with a median lined with Palm trees as far as the eye could see. At the front entrance, in huge gold lettering it read THE DELTONA CORPORATION. Inside, there was an information desk, marbled floors, huge white statues, a waterfall, and four elevators. They toured the inner structure, one floor at a time. The fifth floor was dedicated to computers. Long corridors of computers standing six feet tall with gigantic reels spinning one direction, then the other. The technology was overwhelming!

* * *

Bobby Hardin's condo was in a gated community. It had two bedrooms, a living room with a gas fireplace, a kitchen overlooking the tennis courts, and an attached two-car garage. Two of the walls in the living room were windowed with curtains that opened and closed at the touch of a button.

Bobby's partner, his accountant - was a single female.

Moving from Regency Towers to the condo didn't take very long. Bobby had a lot of friends who were happy to help. He set-up a keg of beer in the garage, and his roommate cooked hot dogs and hamburgers on an outside grill. The move turned into a party!

\* \* \*

The following day, Jerry called. "We are opening a new store in Lima, Ohio next week. It's less than a forty-five minute drive from Cleveland. Can you come down and give me a hand? Ken agreed to pay you in cash."

"I just returned from inspecting nine resort communities in Florida. We are now selling property and housing. And, Gary promoted me to Sales Manager."

"Congratulations! But come down next Saturday anyway. It will be fun. Afterwards, the drinks are on me. The store is on Main Street. You can't miss it."

"I'll try."

The following Saturday Bill parked his El Dorado in front of the store in Lima. Jerry and Ken were both in the back of the store setting up presentation rooms. Hearing the front door open, Jerry walked to the front, saw Bill, and grinned.

"I'm glad you made it!"

When the first appointment arrived, Jerry gave the presentation while Bill watched.

Bill took the second appointment. Six appointments showed up. Jerry closed three, and Bill closed three. Ken paid Bill three hundred dollars in cash, then offered him the managers position at the Lima store.

"That's too far for me to consider."

"Would you be interested in managing a store in Cleveland?" Ken asked.

"That would be a possibility."

"In your travels, start looking for a store location!" Ken smiled.

As they left the store, Bill followed Jerry to the local watering hole.

"Two Crown Royals on the rocks." Jerry told the barmaid as they bellied up to the counter of the bar. The bar reflected the size of the town, it was small. For the most part, Lima, Ohio was an agricultural town with farmers and good down to earth country people trying to earn an honest living. Turning his attention to Bill, Jerry asked. "Well, what do you think now?"

"It was fun!" Bill admitted, not wanting to obligate himself further.

## CHAPTER ELEVEN
## B & H CAMERA

At the next sales meeting, Gary passed out brochures listing the nine resort properties in Florida, and announced. "In addition to the Thursday sales meeting, all sales representatives will be required to attend four weekly training sessions. Details concerning the on-site inspections by potential buyers are not yet available. Check with Celeste next week for an update. Commission will be paid in three increments. The first installment when the contract is signed. The second payment when the ground is broke for construction to be started. And the final payment will be made at closing. I can't give you the precise percentages that will be paid at this time. Study the brochures, learn everything possible about each property, and talk to your friends and associates about these new and exciting resort properties. If a potential client asks you a question, I want you know the answer. You are professionals, act like it!"

After the meeting, Gary called Bill to his office. "You are in-charge of hiring, firing, training, lead control, sales meetings and seminars. You will receive a percentage from every sale made by your sales staff. In addition to that, Celeste has prepared a list of possible leads. Many were previously qualified, but weren't interested in the property in the Bahamas. There are three cardboard boxes sitting in your office filled with potential leads."

Bill sat in his office, looking at the cardboard boxes thinking to himself that nobody, besides himself, was going to sell anything. The sales staff consisted of mostly retirees with nothing better to do. They attended the training and sales meetings, but they merely occupied seats! He thought of his uncle W.A. once telling him. "Son, you can't make a silk purse out of a sow's ear!" He didn't understand what that meant then, but he did now.

"Did you see your name on the door?" Celeste asked, sticking her head into Bill's office?

Bill stood up, looked at the plaque centered on the door.

It read BILL BURNS, SALES MANAGER.

"Office hours are from eight to four. Gary and Don are always here, unless they have an appointment." Celeste offered, smiling.

* * *

The following morning, Bill was standing at his kitchen counter buttering two slices of toast when the phone rang.

"Hello?"

"How are you doing, stranger?" Jerry asked.

"I've been better." Bill sighed his disappointment. "My promotion to Sales Manager just doesn't seem to have a plus side to it. I have my own office which means that I'm expected to spend more time there. There's a ton of added responsibility. I get a percentage of what everyone sells, but nothing from nothing leaves nothing. To top that off, I'm going to be paid in residuals."

"What's that?" Jerry inquired.

"I'm paid in three installments. When the contract is signed. When ground is broke to start the construction. And, at closing."

"Find a location for a store in Cleveland. It's fun, easy money, and at least you know that you won't starve." Jerry chuckled.

"I'll look in Sunday's newspaper. Do you have any idea how much money Ken is expecting to spend?"

"The store in Lima is four hundred and fifty dollars a month, and they signed a six month lease."

After the conversation with Jerry, Bill told Lee about his promotion and all of the added responsibilities that came along with it, adding. "With my being paid residuals, you might want to start looking for a job yourself."

Lee had envisioned himself working for Bill in some capacity, but Octopool was never going to become a reality. Lee had no trade skills, unless you consider safe cracking skilled labor.

* * *

Sunday morning, Bill sat at the kitchen table flipping through the

Cleveland Free Press in search of a store location. One ad caught his attention. Immediate occupancy rent negotiable. The store was located at 11204 Lorain Avenue. Bill called the phone number and after a brief conversation, he made an appointment to inspect the building later that afternoon.

From Regency Towers, it was a twenty minute drive to the store. Lorain Avenue was centrally located. It ran from the city through one suburb after another, past the store, all the way to the Ohio Turnpike. There was easy access to the expressway only two blocks away. The outside of the store was painted yellow and a fifteen foot yellow canvas canopy was centered above the entrance door. The front door was glassed and there were two large windows, one on each side of the door. There was parking permitted on both sides of the street and very little sidewalk traffic outside the store. On the opposite side of the street there was a cemetery with a well cared for lawn and a waist high black wrought iron fence.

The owner of the store was a short Italian who introduced himself as Tony. He spoke broken English, had a fixed smile, a quick laugh, and made a lot of hand gestures. He reminded Bill of an overzealous salesman - quick to make a deal.

The store was empty. The walls were painted yellow, the carpet was plaid - red, black, and green. At the rear of the store, there was a double sided counter with a walk around entrance to the back office area. There was a rear door, and a door that led to a shared basement that could be used for storage. An attorney rented the adjacent office, and he also had a door that opened to the basement. Across the street from the attorneys office was an Irish Pub, the Colonial Boy.

"How much is the rent?"

"Two hundred and fifty dollars a month with a two hundred dollar security deposit." Tony answered.

"Is there a lease requirement?"

"Do you want a lease?" Tony grinned.

"I prefer to rent by the month."

"Sure. No problem. You must pay the utilities too. Gas, and electric."

"Of course!" Bill chuckled, adding. "I'm going to need to make a call before I can make a commitment."

Tony, concerned that Bill may be considering another option, snapped. "Rent today. Two hundred dollars a month, no deposit."

"I'll take it!" Bill smiled, shaking Tony's hand to seal the deal. Century Entertainment should be thrilled with this location, he thought. Bill leaned on the counter, wrote a personal check, and handed it to Tony.

Tony handed Bill two sets of keys, then said. "I will call first, then stop by to pick up the rent on the first of each month."

"That will be fine." Bill smiled his pleasure, and bid Tony a good day.

The store was perfect! The color yellow represented Kodak. The huge yellow canopy made the store visible from a distance. And the expressway made it easily accessible from anywhere in the state. Not to mention, the rent was cheap.

Later that evening Bill called Jerry with the news.

"I'm sure Ken and Jim will be happy to hear that!" Jerry replied, excited by the news.

When Bill told Lee about the store, he was excited too. Lee wanted to see the store right away.

The first thing he noticed was there was no alarm on the front door, and Lee quickly advised Bill to purchase one.

"It would be pretty simple to install. Contacts for the three doors, a motion detector, wiring, and an outside horn. I'd recommend putting a call box in the basement. Radio Shack should have one. If you buy it, I'll install it." Lee offered.

Returning to the apartment, the phone was ringing. Lee answered it. "It's for you, Jerry."

"Hello, big brother."

"Hey! Watch that big brother stuff!" Jerry laughed. "Ken would like for you to come to Dayton Saturday, so that the two of you can sit down and discuss things."

"I'll be there!"

Bonnie called, inviting Bill over for dinner. Karen and Dottie said hello, then disappeared. Bill told Bonnie about his promotion, the added responsibility, and then about the store he rented. After dinner, Bonnie wanted to go see the store.

Twenty-five minutes later, Bill parked the El Dorado at the curb in front of the store. After seeing the store, they strolled down the sidewalk, hand in hand, and into the Irish Pub. There was a huge horseshoe bar open at the back. The bartender smiled, walked over, and said. "Hi Bonnie. What can I get you guys?" as they seated themselves on red leather cushioned stools.

"Hi Raymond. This is my boyfriend, Bill." Bonnie smiled.

Raymond extended his hand in friendship. For his size, he had a firm grip.

"I'll have a Seven and Seven." Bill replied.

"Coke in tall glass with ice." Bonnie snickered.

As Raymond was preparing the drinks, Bonnie told him that Bill had just rented the store two doors down. Then, she explained to Bill that she lived right down the street when she attended college.

"The first drink is on the house!" Raymond announced.

"On Friday and Saturday night this place is packed elbow to elbow. Alex and Mary take the stage and sing Irish songs." Bonnie smiled.

Returning to Bonnie's house, she showed him a shortcut through the city reducing the driving time by a third. With a long passionate kiss goodnight, Bill returned to the apartment.

* * *

It was eight o' clock in the morning. Bill was sitting at the kitchen table sipping a cup of hot coffee while reading the morning paper when Lee walked through the door, and asked. "Where's the van?"

"I parked the El Dorado next to it when I came home last night."

"Well, it's not there now." Lee exclaimed.

"You've got to be shitting me!" Bill retorted, with a sign of disgust.

"It's not there!" Lee repeated.

They inspected where the van had been parked. There was no sign of broken glass, but the van was gone. There was nothing left to do other than make a police report. It had been stolen sometime during the night.

"Do you have insurance?" Lee asked.

"Full coverage. But I'm still going to take a loss. Where are you going to find another 1977 Dodge customized van with less than twenty thousand miles on the odometer?" Bill dreaded the thought of his having to tell Bobby Jenkins.

Lee reported the theft, and the police said they seriously doubted that the van would ever be recovered.

* * *

Since the trip to Dayton was a business meeting and he didn't intend to stay overnight, Bill didn't invite Bonnie. He picked Jerry up at his apartment and they went directly to Century Entertainment.

Ken was sitting on top of a desk with one foot on the floor when they walked into the rear office. He congratulated Bill on a job well done.

Jerry smiled, as if to say I told you so. "There's just one problem." Ken hung his head.

"What's that?" Jerry asked, no longer smiling.

"When I talked to Jim, he reminded me of a bad experience that we had in Cleveland. And, we don't want another store there."

"I have already rented it." Bill snapped.

"This is bullshit!" Jerry said, his face turning beet red.

"I understand. And I apologize for any inconvenience that I may have caused. I have three options to offer you. You can manage the store in Lima."

"Not interested. It's a forty-five minute drive each way."

"Option two. I will reimburse you for the two hundred dollars to cover the first months rent."

''What's option three?" Jerry asked.

"Bill can open the store for himself. For five hundred dollars Century Entertainment will furnish complete packages that will include the camera, projector, and three hundred mailers for the developing of film."

"I'll take option three." Bill announced.

"You are going to open your own store?" Don asked.

"Yes!"

"Well, the first thing that you will need to do is to contact the Bureau of Vital Statistics in Columbus, Ohio and request a copy of their new births for Cuyahoga County. For a small fee they will supply you with the names and addresses who have had new births within the past six months. I suggest you request the stick-on mailing addresses."

Ken handed Bill a postcard that read: Congratulations on your new arrival! You have been selected to receive a brand new Bell and Howell movie camera and projector FREE…if you agree to do your processing with us. Call Ken today at (a phone number was listed) to set-up an appointment.

"When you get a phone, go to a local printer and have postcards made with your name and address on them.

You will also have to make arrangements for customer financing."

"Do you have any extra Kodak boxes, posters, and displays?"

"Sure. There's plenty of that around here."

"I'll take three packages while I'm here. That will give me one to put on display and two to sell." Bill counted out fifteen One hundred dollar bills and handed those to Ken. Then, he and Jerry loaded the El Dorado with the camera packages, boxes, posters, and displays.

The following morning, Bill ordered a phone with two lines. Then, he called the Bureau of Vital Statistics and learned that Cuyahoga County had a population of 2.8 million and five thousand new births a month. The names and addresses on peel and stick on labels would cost two cents each. He ordered the last six months, setting up an account to have the new births sent to him monthly. Bill went to the courthouse to purchase a business license. When the clerk asked for the name of his business, he thought to himself Burns and Hooker, and said. "B & H Camera." Then, he went to a local printer and ordered bright yellow postcards - call Bill Burns today - with the stores phone number.

Two doors down from the printers was Capital Finance Company. Bill introduced himself to the manager, John Stefansky who quickly arranged his customer financing. Bill left Capital Finance with the contracts in his hand.

Bill went on a shopping spree, he bought a folding bronze colored card table with a imitation beige leather top, four matching fold-up chairs, and a yellow five foot plastic divider with open shelves. Bill and Lee spent hours decorating the store.

A local sign maker made a white plastic twelve foot sign.

In black lettering it read B & H Camera, and it was glued to the front of the yellow canopy. It looked very nice. The sign maker was the first to ask if the B & H stood for Bell and Howell.

Next, Bill placed an ad in the Cleveland Free Press for a secretary/receptionist, and he hired Debbie Felker. She was young, thin, and had a friendly phone voice. Debbie lived within walking distance, and most important, she took direction. Bill bought a second hand desk, a secretary chair, and a typewriter. It was Debbie's job to mail out cards, answer the phone, set appointments, and call the contracts in to Capital Finance for approval. She was instructed to schedule appointments after five o' clock on weekdays and afternoon on Saturday.

The Grand opening was scheduled for the following Saturday. Debbie scheduled five appointments, the first one for two o' clock. By seven, Bill had closed on four deals and delivered the equipment to three.

Monday morning Debbie called the contracts in to Capital for approval. All four were approved within an hour. For a check to be issued, Bill had to produce a signed contract with proof of delivery for the merchandise.

Bill called Jerry and told him to have Ken get six camera packages ready. He would be there by eight o' clock that night with the money to pay for the merchandise.

Bill rushed to Capital Finance Company, picked up the checks, then hurried to the Dollar bank to see Vaughn. He deposited the three checks, purchased a Certified check made out to Century Entertainment for three thousand dollars, and opened a business checking account.

After work at Executive, Bill picked Lee up and they drove to Dayton. Bill introduced Lee to Ken and explained that there may be times when Lee will need to make the trip to pick up the camera packages.

## CHAPTER TWELVE
## DAYS OF MADNESS

One month later. At Thursdays sales meeting, Gary reported that he was still waiting for a package to arrive from the Deltona corporation containing the sales kits. At this point, the sales representatives had only been given a few brochures. They had no videos of the properties, contracts, or any other relevant information.

* * *

On the bright side, things were going exceptionally well at B & H Camera. Debbie was mailing out cards every week and setting appointments. Bill was giving sales presentations. In the first month, he closed twenty deals bringing in a gross of twenty thousand dollars.

Going into the second month, he noticed less deals were being approved. It was obvious, at least to Bill, John Stefansky was "cherry picking". John had short brown hair, a mustache, and he was a slim five feet eight. Bill called and invited him to lunch. John dressed casual, and today was no exception. He wore dark blue slacks, a light blue long sleeve shirt, and a modest tie.

Over lunch, Bill bluntly asked. "Why are you cherry picking the contracts?"

John chose his words carefully. "I'm concerned about the sudden rise in volume the office is generating!"

"That doesn't make sense, John. You are in the business of making loans."

"It's not that I don't want the business." John sighed.

"What is it then?" Bill asked, and waited for a response.

"You are a new business, and you came out of the gate swinging. I can't afford to strike out!"

"I don't understand. What exactly do you mean by that?"

"I know very little about your business. What happens if your customers aren't satisfied. You're paid, that leaves your customer not making their payments to us."

"If that's your concern, I will buy back any contract within the first 90-days. But use some discretion. If there's a problem, a hardship, a justifiable reason for me to buy back the contract, I will. You have my Word on that! I am also the Sales Manager for Executive International Development Corporation and I am a member in good standing of the Sales and Marketing Executive's Club of Greater Cleveland."

"That's fair enough!" John smiled, then suggested. "You might want to consider joining the Better Business Bureau."

Debbie opened and closed the store Monday through Saturday. Lee installed an alarm that Bill purchased at Radio Shack. He delivered contracts to Capital Finance Company, picked up checks and deposited them at the Dollar bank.

One Saturday, as Bill opened the door to the basement the door across the hall opened.

"Hi! I'm your neighbor, Mark Knevel the spectacled man spoke extending his hand. Mark was tall, thin, with sandy blonde hair.

"It's nice to finally meet you. I'm Bill Burns. This is my secretary, Debbie. And, my friend Lee."

"I've been dying to know, what kind of business are you in? All I see is people walking out of your store carrying boxes!" he chuckled.

"I sell camera packages. If you agree to develop your film with me, I will give you a FREE Bell & Howell camera and projector."

"Sounds interesting." Mark smiled, as his very pregnant wife peeked her head over his shoulder. "And this is my lovely wife, Cindy." Mark added.

"Hi! Welcome to the neighborhood." Cindy smiled.

"I guess that explains the boxes, the mystery is solved. But I am somewhat disappointed. I hoped for something a little more intriguing, like a drug cartel. Something that might require the services of an attorney."

The phone rang. Debbie answered it. "It's for you, Bill. Someone from The Better Business Bureau."

"Well, it appears that I may be in need of an attorney after all."

"We need the business!" Cindy giggled.

Everyone said their goodbyes and Bill answered the phone. "Hello?"

"Is this Bill Burns?"

"Yes, it is."

"My name is Sue Roshetko and I'm with the Better Business Bureau. I am investigating a complaint filed by a Miss Shiyana Williams. She claims that she received a card in the mail congratulating her on her new arrival and it said that she had been selected to receive a FREE camera and projector, but when she went to pick it up it wasn't free. You must be a new business because we don't yet have a file for you."

"The cards reads 'FREE if you agree to do your processing with us.'"

"So, it's not FREE!"

"It is if you agree to do your developing of film with us. The developing is prepaid in one of three ways. Cash, Visa, or our convenient payment plan which is financed through Capital Finance Company or a financial institution of the customers choice."

"To be absolutely clear, it is not FREE."

"It is not an entitlement. It is not a gift. The card explicitly reads. 'if you agree to develop your film with us.'"

"So, you are going to give Miss Shiyana Williams a FREE camera?"

"That is correct. if she agrees to do her developing of film with us."

"Thank you. Would you be interested in becoming a member of the Better Business Bureau?"

"Yes, I would."

"I will have one of our representatives contact you."

Two weeks later, a wooden plaque was proudly displayed on the wall for customers to see. MEMBER OF THE BETTER BUSINESS BUREAU.

* * *

Bill was a month away from having to renew his lease for another year. Bill called his U.S. Marshall officer to tell him that he was mailing in the last monthly report in his possession, and inform him that he might be moving next month.

"How are things going? "He asked.

"Real good!"

"Well, good luck to you. You're on your own!"

To celebrate his release from parole, Bill took Lee and Debbie to the Colonial Boy, played pool, and drank until closing. "What do you think about us renting a house? If I do that, you could ask your wife and kids to move in." "Are you serious?" Lee beamed.

"I'm going to start looking for a house tomorrow." Bill grinned.

Jenny, Lee's wife had two children. Todd was the oldest, he was six. Although Lee wasn't his biological father, he had raised him as his own. Missy was three, just out of those terrible two's. While Todd was tall, skinny, with coal black hair like his mother. Missy favored Lee. She had brown hair, brown eyes, and she was a daddy's girl.

When Lee called with the news, Jenny was excited. She didn't like living at her mother's house, and hoped this would be a fresh start for them.

Bill rented a house on Center Ridge Road in West Lake, Ohio. It was a huge red brick split level with a two and a-half car garage. It was three bedroom, two and a-half bath, with a Club basement. The foyer was white marble tile imported from Italy, and a winding cherry oak stairway led to the upstairs. Downstairs, there was an elegant dining room, formal living room, den, and a half-bath. Upstairs, there were three bedrooms and two baths. Bill's master bedroom had a Jacuzzi, sauna, tub and shower, and a huge walk -in closet. Patio doors opened to a balcony that had a black wrought iron railing and ran the length of the house. There was a horseshoe driveway with huge white rocks in the yard, and well cared for gardens. In the backyard, there was a swimming pool. The owner was a short Italian who spoke broken English. Bill signed a lease for one year with an option to buy or renew the lease.

* * *

Bill's store and Mark's office were missing one thing, air conditioning. They soon discovered that if they left their backdoors open along with the doors that led to the basement a cool breeze circulated. Debbie and Mark quickly decided to give up their privacy for the shared breeze. When Mark had an appointment with a client, he closed the door. Otherwise, it was open.

With the open door policy, Bill and Mark soon became good friends. Mark was a recent graduate of Notre Dame, and with a baby on the way money was tight. He lived in a modest apartment, and his wardrobe left a lot to be desired. Bill gifted Mark with two new suits and helped furnish his office.

"If I ever need your services, I want you to look your best!" Bill chuckled.

Even so, as nice as he was, Bill was a terrible influence on Mark because he would invite him to lunch, then take him across the street to the Colonial Boy knowing they only served potato chips, beer nuts, and alcoholic beverages.

One afternoon, Mark looked around the store, and commented. "You will take anything in on trade, won't you?" There was a brand new pinball machine in the back of the office, a brand new moped, and an assortment of bottled whisky bottles in antique green and brown glass cars. Mark called Bill "interesting" because he never knew what to expect next.

For Valentine's Day Bill surprised Bonnie with a new car. Well, new to her! It was a metallic brown 1975 Dodge Demon with a vinyl top and tan interior. The car was low mileage and it was equipped with power steering, power brakes, air-conditioning, and a nice stereo. It was in mint condition! Bill hung a sign on the car that read MECHANIC NEEDED - APPLY WITHIN, and parked the car in her driveway. The title was in her name and he had purchased license plates. The title and registration was in the glove compartment, and he placed a huge heart shaped box of chocolate candy in the trunk.

## CHAPTER THIRTEEN
## THE OPPORTUNITY

Lee drove the El Dorado to the airport to pick Jenny and the kids up. At a glance, Bill knew that her heritage was Indian. She was five-seven, with brown eyes, with long coal black hair that fell to her waist. Since she was from the South, Bill guessed that she was Cherokee.

Jenny and the kids loved their new house. From the first day, Missy began calling Bill "Uncle Bill". Missy's bedroom was next to Bill's, and whenever he was at home she always kissed him goodnight. Todd was more reserved. He was quiet and kept to himself. But when asked a question, he always answered "Yes, sir" or "No, sir".

Jenny was quite the Susie Homemaker. She kept the house immaculate, did the laundry, cooked, and worked around the house in the gardens weeding and planting flowers. With curls falling to her shoulders, Missy was a pint size Shirley Temple. Always inquisitive, full of energy, and she brought the life to the house. It now felt like a home.

In the den, there was a huge eight piece pit group, a fireplace centered on a red brick wall, and sliding glass doors that opened to a concrete patio and the backyard.

Jenny was bent over pulling weeds from the flower garden next to the front door, wearing cut-off jeans and a halter top, as Bill pulled into the driveway. Her long black hair shining in the sunlight. Missy was squatting next to her wearing a yellow summer dress and white sandals. "Jerry called." Jenny announced. "He said that Ken wants you to attend a ten o' clock meeting Monday morning, and that all of the store managers are required to be there."

Before Jenny came to live at the house, Lee was friends with a girl that he met at the Colonial Boy, Nancy DeLorean. Nancy was tall, thin, with brown hair - just the opposite of Jenny. Nancy's passion was horses and she invited Lee and Bill to watch her ride in a rodeo. Her father was a successful businessman, he owned DeLorean Cadillac which was two blocks from B & H Camera. In his showroom, there was a silver gull-winged DeLorean.

It was claimed to be the first one off of the assembly line - a gift from his brother, John DeLorean. Friday night Bill sold out of camera packages. His plan was to pick up six packages after the Monday morning sales meeting.

Saturday morning everyone climbed into the El Dorado to go for a ride around the lake and through the Park. Being new to the area, Jenny hadn't had the opportunity to see very much. As they drove by a new car Chevrolet dealership, through the display window a white Trans-Am with a decal of a huge Eagle on the hood caught Bill's eye. It was gorgeous! Fancy white rims, t-tops, raised white letter tires. Bill did a U-turn, drove into the lot of the dealership, parked, and walked inside. It was a brand new 1981 Chevrolet Trans-Am. It was a limited edition, known as the Indy Pace Car. White leather seats with checkered black and white panels and a dash that glowed reddish pink lighting up the instrument panel. Three yellow lights molded into the hood lit-up left to right as the turbo kicked in. The Trans-Am came equipped with an automatic transmission, tilt wheel, cruise control, air-conditioning, power windows, mirrors, seats, and glass smoked t-tops.

"I gotta have it!" Bill grinned.

"You're crazy." Jenny giggled.

"Maybe so. But in that car, I'll look good being crazy."

Ten minutes later, Bill was in the salesman's office filling out a credit application.

"Do you think your credit will be approved?" Lee asked, hopefully. Lee knew that if Bill's credit was approved, he would be driving the El Dorado.

"I won't know until Monday. By the way, there's a car show at the Convention Center through the weekend. Anybody interested in going to that?"

"I wanna go, uncle Bill!" Missy shouted.

"You want to go to everything, don't you?" Jenny giggled. Missy nodded her head in agreement. Bill called the salesman, his credit was approved and he picked up the new Trans-Am.

\* \* \*

After breakfast, Lee grabbed his camera announcing they would need to stop and purchase more film before they went inside the Convention Center. They parked in a underground parking lot in downtown Cleveland. It was the most convenient and closest parking to the Convention Center.

The cars and trucks on display were awesome. There was every Make, Model, and color conceivable not to mention the prototypes. Sections roped off displayed car polishes, waxes, rims and tires. Then, there were booths advertising house windows, vinyl siding, heating and air-conditioning. All types of merchandise.

One booth caught Bill's attention, more than any of the others. Two young girls dressed in shorts and halter-tops were selling ice-cream on a stick. An elderly gray hair man stood at a folding table behind the girls slicing gallons of vanilla ice-milk with a long knife into eighteen slices. Then, he inserted a thin flat stick into each slice, placed them on a cookie sheet pan and passed the ice-milk to the girls. They dipped the sliced ice-milk into a crock pot of chocolate, rolled it in a pan of crushed nuts, wrapped a napkin around the stick, and charged the customer One dollar. There were two long lines of customers. Bill mentally did the math, eighteen dollars for maybe, at the most, a five dollar investment. That was one smart old man, he chuckled to himself.

* * *

Sunday night Bill called Jerry, and said. "I'll meet you at Century Entertainment around nine o' clock in the morning."

That was fine with Jerry. Bright and early Monday morning Bill showered, shaved, dressed, and left the house on his way to Dayton, Ohio.

The meeting lasted for thirty minutes and absolutely nothing applied to Bill. Highly irritated, Bill asked Ken. "Exactly why did I need to be here?"

"Because you are operating your store under the wing of Century Entertainment. Your camera packages include our mailers for your film processing, so the same rules that apply to other stores also apply to you, which include attending the monthly sales meeting. "

Accepting Ken's explanation, Bill asked for the six camera packages he ordered.

The six packages were already prepared and stacked near the front entrance. As Bill started to write Ken a check from B & H Camera's business account, Ken abruptly announced. "Sorry, but we don't accept personal checks."

"It's a business check!" Bill declared.

"Our policy is that we only accept certified checks, and cash."

"You're not going to accept a check from my brother!" Jerry screamed.

"It's our Policy." Ken stood his ground, making no exceptions.

"You could have told me this before now. How was I expected to go the bank in Cleveland and be in Dayton by ten o'clock?"

Ken shrugged his shoulders, offering no response.

Jerry was livid. He looked at Ken, then back at the floor, and bit his lip.

"That's fine." Bill retorted. He grabbed Jerry and walked him back to one of the rear offices. "Nothing good can come from either of us blowing up!"

"How much cash do you have on you?" Jerry asked. As he counted the money in his pocket, Bill noticed the secretary, sitting at her desk, was sorting through a box of mail containing Century Entertainment mailers. As she removed the film from the envelope, she logged an entry, then placed the customer's film in another envelope to be mailed for processing. The phone rang. After answering the call, the secretary left her desk for a minute. While she was gone, Bill took the opportunity to take one of the mailers and pocket it. Leaving the store, Bill told Ken that he would return with the cash. After a quick trip to Jerry's bank, Bill returned and paid cash for the six camera packages.

On his trip back to Cleveland Bill pulled the mailer from his pocket, inspecting it. It was a prepaid mailer purchased from the 3-M Company.

Bill recalled the time he purchased jewelry at Best Products. There was an entire department filled with camera equipment. All of the name brands, including Bell & Howell. Returning to Cleveland, he stopped at a Best Products store in Parma. It was well stocked with Bell & Howell cameras and projector's at wholesale prices.

Bill stopped at the store to unload the camera packages. Debbie announced. "I've set two appointments for tonight. One at five-thirty, the other is at six forty-five.

* * *

A month later, Ken called to inform Bill of a sales meeting that he would be required to attend.

"There's no reason for me to attend. B & H Camera is no longer associated with Century Entertainment."

"I was wondering why you hadn't purchased any camera packages in awhile. I didn't think business was that bad."

"Business has been exceptionally good."

"Well, good luck to you." Ken said.

"Good luck to you too." Bill replied.

Two weeks later, Jerry quit Century Entertainment and moved to Shamburg, a suburb of Chicago. Lynn found work as a secretary, while Jerry took a job selling freight.

"Debbie, call Bell & Howell. I would like to speak with a representative."

Bill made an appointment for a representative to visit the store the following Tuesday at two o'clock.

Bill sat in a chair across from Debbie's desk and thumbed through the Yellow pages. "I think it's time to buy some furnishings," he announced, looking for Debbie's reaction. She simply smiled. He located a company downtown that sold new and used office equipment and restaurant supplies and called for directions. At the store Bill purchased three white used six feet lighted display cases. They were four feet high. The front, top, and shelves were glass. At the rear, there were sliding doors for easy access. Then, he purchased a nice secretary desk and comfortable chair for Debbie, along with a typewriter and IBM copier.

The following day, the furniture was delivered. Bill and Lee ran one display case sideways to the wall, and two lengthwise. This allowed for a three and a-half foot walkway behind the counter. It looked fantastic, but noticeably bare.

Bill stopped at Modern Camera, a camera store about a mile away. They welcomed the business, offering to sell Bill merchandise at wholesale prices and gifting him with a display cabinet for Kodak film, two side foot racks, and some colorful posters and memorabilia. Bill purchased some film, an assortment of new and used 35 millimeter cameras, and ten large brown imitation leather carrying cases.

At a sidewalk sale, Bill purchased wood framed colorful photos of tigers, exotic birds, and antique cars.

From a Florist, he purchased two potted trees along with several hanging plants.

When the store was completed, it no longer looked-like a paper store. Debbie had appointments scheduled for the following night. "I almost forgot." Debbie said. "Some guy has been calling for you. He wouldn't leave his name, but he said that he was from Consumer Affairs."

"Call the Convention Center and reserve the largest booth available for the Sportsman's Show." Bill replied, unconcerned about some guy calling from Consumer Affairs.

## CHAPTER FOURTEEN
## THE SPORTSMAN'S SHOW

The next day the overnight delivery arrived from the 3-M Company, and Bill bought Debbie a book to keep a record of every mailer she received and remailed to the 3-M Company. The process was simple, but she needed to keep an accurate account for the mailings. In the next few days, Bill closed eight deals delivering the equipment to his customers. He presented the contracts to Capital Finance and an individual check was issued for each purchase. True to his Word, Bill bought back one contract at John's request. The woman's husband was killed in an auto accident and she had fell on hard times.

The phone rang, and Debbie answered it. "It's for you, Bill. That guy from Consumer Affairs."

"Hello?" Bill answered.

"Is this Bill Burns?"

"Yes, it is. How may I help you?"

"My name is Bryant. I'm an agent for Consumer Affairs. Before we file a Complaint in court, we would like to extend an olive branch to you. An opportunity for you to make an appointment to come to our office and discuss the Complaint."

"I wasn't aware of there being a Complaint!" Bill replied, nonchalantly.

"I am looking at a yellow card with your name on it that reads: CONGRATULATIONS ON YOUR NEW ARRIVAL. YOU HAVE BEEN SELECTED TO RECEIVE A FREE BELL & HOWELL MOVIE CAMERA AND PROJECTOR TODAY - IF YOU AGREE TO DO YOUR PROCESSING WITH US. CALL BILL BURNS TODAY FOR AN APPOINTMENT. Is that your card?"

"Yes, it is."

"Well, we have a Complaint filed by a Miss Shaniya Williams who claims that she made an appointment, went to your store to receive her FREE Bell & Howell movie camera and projector to discover that it wasn't FREE at all."

"It is, if you agree to do your processing. with us. That's clearly what the card reads."

"I'm not going to debate this issue with you over the phone. Would you like the opportunity to set an appointment to come into the office and discuss this, or not?"

"Set the appointment and I'll be there!"

"What is better for you. Mornings, or afternoons?"

"Late afternoon would be better for me."

"How about next Thursday at four o'clock?"

"I'll see you then!" Bill said, and hung up.

The basement doors were open, so Bill crossed into Mark's office, and asked. "What are you doing next Thursday afternoon?"

Mark looked at his weekly Planner, then replied. "Nothing! Why are you asking?" "Because I have an appointment at Consumer Affairs, and I would like for you to go with me."

"Sure, no problem. What's it about?" Mark inquired.

"Some girl first complained to the Better Business Bureau that I was falsely advertising a FREE Bell & Howell movie camera and projector. When she wasn't satisfied with their finding, she contacted Consumer Affairs." Bill showed Mark one of the cards. "It clearly states IF YOU AGREE TO DO YOUR PROCESSING WITH US. As I explained to the Better Business Bureau, it's not an entitlement, or gift!"

"This should be fun." Mark chuckled. That night Mark's wife Cindy had a baby boy. Jesse Knevel was born into the world. Cindy spent most of her time at the office answering the phone, setting appointments, typing, and doing whatever needed to be done. With her in the hospital, Mark was going be under a lot more pressure. But, when Cindy was able, she would be bringing the newborn to work.

Tuesday Bill met with the representative from Bell & Howell. He was impressed with the store and took a personal liking to Bill. He requested that Bell & Howell give B & H Camera a fifty thousand dollar line of credit.

Thursday, Bill and Mark walked into the office of Consumer Affairs and asked to see Bryant. He was tall, thin, and wore horn rimmed glasses. Bill introduced himself, then Mark as his attorney.

"I'm not sure if I will need legal advice." Bill explained.

"That's fine. May I see some identification?"

"Sure!" Bill opened his wallet and produced his Ohio drivers license.

"I'm surprised." Bryant exclaimed.

"What surprises you?" Bill asked, out of curiosity.

"In most cases, the name on the card doesn't reflect an actual person."

"Is your name really, Bryant?" Bill inquired.

"For our own protection, we don't use our real names. I have checked with the Better Business Bureau and you are a member. If you will follow me into my office, we will discuss the Complaint."

As Bill and Mark sat down, Mark opened his brief case, took out a yellow legal pad, removed a gold pen from his shirt pocket, and immediately began taking notes.

"The Complaint is filed by who?" Mark asked.

"A Miss Shaniaya Williams. "

"Everybody advertises something for FREE, but it's always conditional." Bill voiced his thoughts.

Mark agreed, giving an example that Sears advertises that if you purchase five glasses, the sixth one is FREE.

"And Pizza Hut, Burger King, McDonalds. Buy one, get one FREE. They all do the same thing." Bill added.

"We are not here to debate Sears, Pizza Hut, McDonalds, or Burger King. Should this case proceed to court, you may wish to argue those points in your defense. The dilemma that I'm dealing with is that YOU advertise a FREE camera and projector and it's clearly not FREE. "

"What if I substituted the word FREE with NO CHARGE, the card would read, NO CHARGE IF YOU AGREE TO DO YOUR PROCESSING WITH US."

"I think that would be acceptable." Bryant grinned.

"I wouldn't agree to that! I have no problem taking this to court." Mark said, sitting upright.

"I really don't want to go through the hassle." Bill grinned. I don't

believe that changing the wording is going to affect the business. I'll give
it a try!"

As they walked to the El Dorado, Mark repeated. "I wouldn't have
agreed to that!"

"I didn't agree to anything." Bill grinned, correcting Mark. "I said that I
would give it a try. If it doesn't work, then I will go back to using the word
FREE."

Mark laughed heartily. Bill's logic amused him.

* * *

The next morning when Bill walked into the office he had a surprise
visitor, the representative from Bell & Howell. "I hope you don't mind my
stopping in unannounced, but I was in the area and I have some news for
you. Bell & Howell did not approve your application for a credit line of fifty
thousand dollars. But they did approve you for a twenty thousand dollar
line of credit." He smiled.

Bill immediately placed an order for fifty Bell & Howell movie cameras
and projectors. A week later the delivery truck parked at the front door. Lee
and Bill began stacking boxes one on top of another. There was a massive
amount of inventory!

Don Conley stopped by the store. He couldn't believe his eyes. The
store had grown dramatically since his first visit.

* * *

Jerry called. He had recently opened a video store in Shamburg with two
partners, and he was anxious for Bill to come visit. A competitor advertised
the only thing their customers needed was the popcorn. So Jerry bought a
popcorn machine on wheels and advertised a FREE bag of popcorn with
every video rental. Jerry chuckled, and said. "The smell of freshly popped
corn seems to boost business!"

Bill called Bonnie and asked. "How would you like to spend Christmas in Chicago with Jerry, and Lynn?"

"Are you asking me to go with you?" Bonnie giggled.

"Yeah! I guess I am." Bill chuckled.

"Then, I would absolutely love to spend Christmas in Chicago. I thought you had been avoiding me."

"No, I haven't. Things have just been hectic lately." After talking for the better part of an hour, they decided on having a beer ball game on Saturday. Invite all of their friends and put quarter kegs on first, second, and third - with shots of Schnapps at home plate. Dottie quickly volunteered to hand out the shots.

Saturday was a beautiful day. Mark and Cindy, Bobby Hardin, Bill and Bonnie, Lee and Jenny - along with Dottie and Karen's friends were all there to have a good time.

Bill went downstairs and raided Bonnie's closet for hats. As he passed them out, Bonnie yelled. "I want them back at the end of the game!"

By the third inning everyone was pretty wasted. They gathered around a picnic table and grabbed hot dogs and hamburgers from the grill.

* * *

The following day, Bill went to JCPenny's and purchased matching beige sport jackets for himself, Lee, and Debbie. Then, he went to a trailer and had B&H embroidered on a brown shield in gold letters, and sewn onto the jacket's upper left pocket.

After that he went to his signmaker and ordered a gold and brown sign to hang above his booth at the Sportsman's Show.

Stopping at Modern Camera, he purchased a front screen projector. This completed his presentation for the Sportsman's Show.

* * *

The Sportsman's show was everything Bill had hoped for, and more. The booth stood out and people stopped to inquire about the FREE cameras and projectors. Bill wrote twelve contracts with delivery upon approval. Ten were approved!

B&B Marine  had a nice display of boats. As Bill stood admiring a 1981 23' metallic brown Bayliner, the owner of the business Bill Fannon introduced himself.

Bill filled out a credit application to purchase the Bayliner. The boat had a 230 Chrysler inboard/outboard motor, a cuddy cabin, beige leather captain chairs, a matching sun deck, and full canvas with windows on the side. There was a hatch, a chrome railing going around the front of the bow, and a stereo system. And the boat had a top speed of sixty miles an hour.

"I'm not sure if my credit will be approved."

"Well, if it is I will pay for a year for you to dock the boat at Anchor's-Away in Port Clinton. It's an hours drive from Toledo but it has easy access to the islands."

Put-in Bay and Kelly's island were both within a mile of the dock.

Bill's credit application was approved the next day.

## CHAPTER FIFTEEN
## ANCHOR'S AWAY

Bill's brand new Bayliner was docked at Anchor's Away in Port Clinton, at the very end of the dock on the right. There was indoor storage offered for the winter months. On the premises there was a nice restaurant, a bait and tackle shop, a boat ramp, and a gravel lot with ample parking.

In good weather, Kelly's island was a fifteen minute boat ride. There were eateries on the island, two hotels, a campground, several bars, hiking trails, and bike rentals. The sidewalks were planked, and local venders pushed hot dog and ice-cream carts down the dirt roads.

Put-in-Bay featured a winery with tours. The favored part of that was the wine tasting experience.

B & B Marine was only three miles from the marina. Going to and from Anchor's Away, Bill drove past Bill Fannon's business, and if Bill's black Trans-Am was parked in front of the business, he would always stop to say hello. On one occasion, Bill Fannon invited Bill home for dinner. Parked in his driveway was a white Trans-Am. He explained that when he bought his Trans-Am, he bought a matching white one for his wife. Bill Fannon was an avid gun collector. Pistol's, still in the box, were tucked away beneath the couch in his living room. Racks and racks of polished rifles stood upright in locked mahogany glass display cases.

Bill had two photos taken standing in front of a red brick fireplace. In one, he held a pair of matching nickel plated, pearl handled Colt .45's. In the other photo, one hand was on the stock, the other on the trigger of a Thompson .45 caliber machine gun. A switch on the side converted it from fully to semi automatic.

That night Bill went bar hopping with Bill Fannon, only to learn that he loved to fight and was barred from most of the bars.

On one outing, Bill took Lee and his family to Kelly's Island. At the dock, he started the boat's engine, unbuttoned the canvas and exposed the entire boat to the sun. It was a beautiful day with a mild breeze. Lee untied the ropes securing the boat and tossed them onto the dock, and they were soon out of the inlet and into the open waters of Lake Erie. Bill pushed the throttle forward until the boat reached its top speed.

"Slow down. You're scaring the kids!" Jenny yelled.

Bill and Lee both laughed. As soon as Jenny sat down in the boat she tied a life preserver around the kids' necks, then hers. It was Jenny who was afraid.

"I wish we had some water skis." Bill said.

On the return home to Cleveland, a State Trooper on the opposite side of the median hit his brakes. Bill looked down at the speedometer, the Eldorado was pushing ninety miles an hour. The Trooper, unable to find the place to turn around, radioed ahead for another trooper to stop the silver Eldorado. Bill passed an exit. He thought about exiting, but he didn't. A half mile further down the road a trooper parked alongside the road pulled out, fell in behind the El Dorado, and turned it's overheads on.

Bill pulled to the side of the road and when the Trooper approached, he asked. "Can I help you, officer?"

"Two and a-half miles back you were clocked at eighty-eight miles an hour."

"There must be some mistake." Bill replied.

"No mistake! 1978-79 silver El Dorado with two males and a female in the front seat, the female has black hair. May I see your drivers license, registration, and proof of insurance?"

Bill cooperated with the Trooper's request. As he read the ticket, the cost was sixty dollars.

The next day Bill asked Mark if he would go to court with him. "What's your defense?"

"They got the wrong guy." Bill chuckled.

"Oh! That should be interesting. I guess you know that you're buying lunch."

"Of course." Bill grinned. He didn't care about the sixty dollars, it was the points that he didn't want.

That night, Bill closed the Colonial Boy. As he walked to the El Dorado, he noticed a light in the rear of the store. The front door was locked, but the alarm wasn't turned on. He unlocked the door, walked to the back office, and found Debbie sitting at her desk in tears.

"What's wrong?" Bill asked. "My sister moved in with her boyfriend and I don't have anywhere else to go."

"Yes, you do. We'll work it out." Bill replied, telling her to gather her things.

"Where are we going?" Debbie asked.

"To the house, for now. You can sleep on the pit group in the den and Lee will drive you back and forth to work."

Bill turned the lights off, locked the front door, and turned the alarm on with a twist of a small tubular key. Within minutes the Trans-Am turned the corner, making a right. They drove by DeLorean Cadillac on the left. Through the showroom window the silver gull-wing DeLorean was clearly visible. They went over the overpass, turned left onto the on ramp of the expressway. Bill pressed the gas pedal to the floor and watched the three yellow lights on the hood come to life.

On Center Ridge Road Bill turned left into the horseshoe driveway of the huge red brick split foyer home. He parked the Trans-Am in the driveway near the front entrance. The porch lights were on, and a dim light in the foyer. Bill opened the front door with Debbie following closely behind him.

Once inside the house, he gave Debbie a blanket and pillow. She took off her shoes, curled up covering herself with the blanket, and quickly fell asleep. How long had she been at the store crying, he wondered.

Debbie was a quiet shy girl and easy to like. Jenny was the first to wake up and find Debbie asleep in the den. As she began cooking breakfast for the kids, Debbie sat up.

"Hi stranger. Are you hungry?" Jenny smiled.

"Do you have any coffee?"

"Sure do. How do you like yours?"

"Cream and two sugars, thank you." Debbie replied, then asked. "Where's the bathroom?"

"Use the one upstairs. It's a full bath. Go up the stairs, turn right, first door on the left."

"Thank you." Debbie smiled.

\* \* \*

Thursday, at Executive International Development Corporation Gary asked to speak with Bill after the sales meeting.

"Are you planning to stay with us? I've heard that you have a new business and I understand if you might not have the time to fill both shoes."

"I loved selling the property in the Bahamas. But the added responsibility of being promoted to Sales Manager, the undertaking of nine resort properties in Florida, and being paid residuals. It would probably be better for the both of us if I resign my position"

"Well, good luck in your new endeavor. I wish you much success."

"Thank you, Gary. So far, the business has exceeded my expectations."

Bill gathered his personal belongings, said goodbye to Don Conley and Celeste, and closed the office door behind him.

That marked the end of Bill's association with Executive International Development Corporation.

\* \* \*

Bonnie's lease was up on the house. She rented an upstairs apartment five blocks from the store. Bobby Hardin offered the use of one his cube trucks and he, Lee, and Bill moved her. The second floor apartment was up a steep narrow stairway.

"Couldn't you find an apartment with just a few more steps." Bill complained.

No one had ever paid attention to how much stuff Bonnie had accumulated until that day. The one thing she didn't have was a television. So, Bill went to the store and bought her a brand new 19" RCA television. It was only black and white, but she didn't care. Bonnie was excited and happy.

* * *

In Sandusky, Mark went to court with Bill for the ticket. Mark and the prosecutor disappeared into the judges chambers. Mark came out laughing, and said. "Let's go!"

"What's so funny?" Bill asked.

"The clerk has been trying to get in touch with you for a week - to no avail. The judge said that if you paid the ticket, he wouldn't report it, so there would be no points against your drivers license. Because you didn't return the call, they thought that you were bringing some hot shot attorney to challenge their radar. And the judge is a former pilot who knows all about radar. When I told them that your defense was going to simply be they stopped the wrong guy, they laughed."

Bill paid the ticket, then took Mark to lunch.

* * *

Don Conley brought a millionaire businessman from Corpus Christie, Texas to the store. Ralph Gutman was so impressed with Bill's store that he offered to buy all of the merchandise, move Bill to Corpus Christie and pay him five hundred dollars a week plus commission to manage a store for him. Ralph said that he would open his own finance company and have a first class operation. Respectfully, Bill declined the offer. He reasoned that he was earning more than twenty thousand dollars a month with one store. His vision was to expand.

# CHAPTER SIXTEEN
## CHRISTMAS IN CHIGAGO

Bonnie's bags were packed, and she thoughtfully filled a cooler with sandwiches and Coca-Cola. Bill had decided to drive the El Dorado, there was more room for luggage and it would be more comfortable. Bill picked Bonnie up, then stopped by his house in Westlake. The split level red brick home was 3 bedroom with an attached 2 ½ car garage with a horseshoe driveway off Center Ridge road. In the center of the driveway was a huge white boulder and a rose garden. Bill parked near the front door. Jenny busied herself pulling weeds from the garden by the front step.

"It's beautiful!" Bonnie announced, taking in a deep breath to smell the sweetness of the roses.

"It's a lot of upkeep." Bill grinned.

Jenny burst into laughter. "Like you really do a lot of work around here."

It was true. Bill never mowed the grass, cleaned the pool, weeded the gardens, or helped with the housework. He paid the bills. Bonnie and Jenny quickly became best friends.

Within the hour Bill and Bonnie were on the Ohio Turnpike 80/90 West to Chicago.

It was Bill's first time driving through the Windy City. There was traffic everywhere - under, over, and on both sides of the El Dorado. It was a massive wave of roads, cars and trucks bumper to bumper, with maniac's weaving from one lane to another honking their horns. Skyscrapers towered the sky, and thick dark smoke poured from the stacks of factories. Below them, a waterway showed small wakes from boats tiny in the distance and huge ships anchored at the docks. On the face of a building, a clock read two-thirty.

On the far side of Chicago, there were two exits for Shamburg. Jerry's directions were for Bill to take the second exit, and it looped to a street. Bill turned right and drove five miles counting the red lights. He drove past a small shopping center, turned left into an apartment complex and directly in front of them was Jerry and Lynn's apartment. Jerry had traded Lynn's canary 1977 Coupe Deville in on a new Volkswagon convertible. It was a special edition, fully loaded. The bronze Cimmaron Volkswagon convertible was parked in the driveway. Bill pulled in beside it, parked, and honked the horn.

Jerry and Lynn stepped out of the apartment to greet Bill and Bonnie, smiling.

"Did you have any trouble finding the apartment?" Jerry asked.

"The directions were easy to follow." Bill said, giving Lynn an affectionate hug.

"How was your trip?" Lynn asked.

"Good, except for the traffic." Bonnie answered.

"You're lucky that you didn't drive through the City of Chicago during the rush hour." Jerry chuckled.

"It gets worse?" Bill frowned. "You have no idea how bad it gets. The people in the Windy City are always in a hurry to get to wherever they're going."

The apartment was small, but cozy. The front door entered into the kitchen, the dining room had sliding glass doors that opened to a small concrete patio.

To the left, was the living room with a stairway leading upstairs to the bedroom and one full bath. It was comfortably furnished with a Christmas tree in one corner beautifully decorated with presents neatly stacked beneath it.

Bill looked to the opposite corner, next to the sliding glass door was Ralph. Alive, and well!

Jerry was anxious to leave. He wanted to introduce Bill and Bonnie to a small karaoke bar that he claimed sold the best wing dings in Chicago - and maybe the world.

"Chicago is nuts!" Bonnie reported.

"Shamburg isn't too bad, but I hate driving in the City." Lynn admitted.

"I don't think that I'd want to live here." Bill surmised. Jerry put the top down and they drove the Volkswagon Cimmaron downtown. To get to the bar they had to park, then walk down a red brick street with trees growing out of the sidewalk. The small bar was on their left. As they entered, people were taking turns at the microphone in the hopes of their being discovered by a roving talent scout.

Jerry ordered a pitcher of beer and a large plate of spicy wing dings for everyone.

"The wings are very good." Bill admitted, biting into a second one.

Bonnie agreed.

Some of the singers were amazingly talented, while others were booed off the stage. Bill and Jerry were working on their third pitcher of beer when Lynn frowned and said that she was ready to leave.

Bonnie concurred. "Killsports!" Bill blurted out - whatever that meant. Jerry wondered if there even was such a word.

After leaving the bar, Jerry drove to a run down section of the City, and said. "I gotta show you this!" As he pulled up to a corner, street dealers rushed the car offering hash, cocaine, heroin, marijuana - a variety of drugs. Jerry bought a half ounce of marijuana.

Jerry dropped the girls at the apartment, then drove to the video store. It was in a small shopping center. In the front were two large picture windows, one on each side of the glass entrance door. Inside, there was a cubed area and a cash register for the clerks. To the right of the front entrance stood a windowed popcorn machine on wheels with a stainless steel bucket that popped the corn, then tilted to empty the popped corn into the large container. There were six aisles with shelves of videos for rent, and sale. It was a first class operation, Bill thought.

Back at the apartment, Jerry had five Tupperware bowls in his refrigerator, each filled with a different type of marijuana. Mood adjusters, he called them. Bill and Jerry were a terrible influence on Bonnie, the bong was a new experience for her!

After placing the presents that Bill and Bonnie brought under the tree, Lynn handed them blankets and pillows and they camped out in the living room. The next morning when Jerry and Lynn walked down the stairs Bill and Bonnie were sitting on the floor playing backgammon.

Everyone opened their presents. Jerry had bought him and Bill matching medallions for the gold chains, the medallions were made from Pikes Peak gold. Bonnie had made Jerry a picture of Mickey Mouse giving the middle finger and framed it. Jerry loved it!

After lunch, they said their goodbyes. Bill did not want to get caught in the rush hour traffic.

Arriving back in Cleveland, Bill dropped Bonnie at her apartment, then drove to the house. Lee was happy to see the El Dorado pulling into the driveway. He preferred driving it.

\* \* \*

When Bill moved into the house, he returned the rented furniture, purchasing everything brand new. In his bedroom he had a king size bed with a hand carved headboard made of red cedar, with the best mattress money could buy. He swore that he would never own another waterbed! His walk-in closet had shelves on both sides. One half of the closet was filled with suits, sport coats, and leather jackets. The other half consisted of dress shirts and slacks on hangers. One shelf had an assortment of sweaters were piled high. On the other, folded jeans. A rack was filled with polished shoes. And on the floor was a variety of tennis shoes and sandals.

Bill was always getting job offers. Word of his leaving Executive International had spread. One morning, he received a call asking if he would be interested in managing the Harley Inn near the airport. The motel had a restaurant, and nightclub. It was an early call, and Bill suggested the caller call back. There was never a second call.

B & H Camera opened at 10 o'clock in the morning and closed at five o' clock if there were no appointments.

Monday morning, Lee drove Debbie to the store. She had just finished brewing a fresh pot of coffee when Bill arrived. Lee was standing at the pinball machine, playing a game by himself.

\* \* \*

"Did you have a good time in Chicago?" Lee asked, with a sly grin.

"Great time! Have you ever been to Chicago?" Bill asked.

"Nope."

"It's insane! I've never seen roads go under and over each other. It's like a pretzel." Bill declared, adding. "And the people drive like maniacs."

Debbie giggled.

"How's Jerry?" Lee inquired.

"He's doing good. He has a video store that's really quite impressive."

The phone rang. Debbie answered it. "It's for you, Bill."

Bill took the receiver and said. "Hello?"

"Hello, Bill?" The caller asked.

"Yes! How may I help you?"

"My name is Rich Richards. I've heard nothing but good things about you and I'd like to get together with you and talk about a proposition that I think you will be interested in."

"What's that?" Bill asked, not wanting to waste his time.

"I would prefer that you come to my house, take a look at what I have to offer, and then decide whether or not you want to be a part of it."

"That sounds fair enough." "When would be a good time for you?"

"Where do you live?" Bill asked.

"Mayfield Heights."

Bill was familiar with the area, it was about a forty-five minute drive from the store. "How about seven o'clock?"

"That works for me." Rich said, giving directions.

To make a better first impression, Bill drove the El Dorado. Rick lived in a two story white brick home with a two and a-half car attached garage. Three vehicles were parked in the driveway. A blue Ford truck, a red foreign compact, and a new white Chevrolet Blazer.

Greeting Bill at the door, Rich quickly ushered him to the basement. There were maps, models, brochures, and blue prints spread over a long wooden table.

"Bill, this is my father. Rich Richards, Sr."

Rich and his father had the same features. His father's hair was a little grayer, but they were the same height and weight. And, they both dressed casual.

"The reason that we brought you here is because we wanted you to see our plans to build condos on Great Exuma. My father and I have mortgaged our homes and invested every penny in this project. That's how much we believe in the concept."

"Concept? What exactly is it that you intend to do?"

"Let me show you."

Rich opened a colorful brochure showing what the condos would look like once they were built. Two bedrooms, kitchen, living room, one bath with an attached carport. Completely furnished, including a car.

"The condo's aren't for sale. We intend to sell "time shares". The client can purchase one or two weeks a year, for life. If they join the Club, they can switch their time for a condo in another resort area. Imagine vacationing in the Bahamas one year, Mexico the next for a small fee." Bill felt that was going to be a hard sale. He could not imagine anyone buying "a time share". In hindsight, it was the biggest mistake of his life. He passed on the opportunity to be the Sales Manager of a multi-million dollar business.

* * *

One night after work, Bill took Debbie to the Colonial Boy. They played pool, drank, laughed and joked until closing. The following morning Debbie walked out of Bill's bedroom wearing nothing but one of his long sleeve shirts.

Jenny stepped out of her bedroom, saw Debbie, suddenly appeared in the doorway of Bill's room, and said. "You should be ashamed of yourself!"

After breakfast, Lee drove Debbie to work. When Bill left the house, he stopped at the BP gas station at the corner, filled the gas tank of the Trans-Am, purchased a map of the state of Ohio, and drove to the store.

As he walked through the store, the smell of fresh coffee brewing filled his nostrils. All of the doors were open. Mark and Cindy were in Mark's office with baby Jesse in a basinet next to the desk, sleeping peacefully.

"He's growing like a weed!" Bill said, playing with his tiny fingers.

"Shush! Don't you wake him." Cindy pleaded.

"I haven't slept all night since he came home." Mark sighed.

"Neither have I!" Cindy was quick to point out.

"How much is it going to cost me to incorporate?" Bill asked Mark.

"Somewhere between four hundred and fifty and five hundred and fifty dollars depending on the amount of stocks and bonds you purchase."

"I'm thinking about opening a second store."

"Where?" Mark asked.

Debbie, Lee, and Cindy looked at Bill waiting for a response. "I don't know yet." Bill chuckled. "I just bought a map of Ohio." As he looked at the map, Toledo stood out. It was only an hour and a-half drive. The day was early and the gas tank was full. Bill removed the t-tops, turned the stereo up, and cruised. He stopped at the toll booth at the Ohio Turnpike, grabbed a ticket, and got off at Exit 5 At a 76 Truck Stop Bill purchased a local map of Toledo and picked up the newspaper, the days edition of the local Toledo Blade. In the restaurant he ordered a hot roast beef sandwich with gravy on the fries and a Coca-Cola.

He browsed through the Want Ads in search of a store to rent. There were two possibilities. One on Lagrange Street, the other at 1837 Alexis Road. His waitress said the store on Alexis would probably be the better location. Then, she gave directions.

"Take 280 to 75 North. The second exit will be Alexis Road. Turn left!"

On Alexis Road he drove past the Greenwood Mall on his right, a car wash, a small shopping center, a GM factory, a Midas muffler shop, and several small bars. Stopped at a red light, the crossroad was Jackman Road. K-Mart had entrances from Alexis and Jackman. Directly in front of K-Mart there was an office building and the address was 1837 West Alexis. A sign in front read, Office space for rent with a phone number.

Bill pulled into the parking lot, and parked. To the left, there was a Realty company. He opened the front door walking down the corridor of the air-conditioned building. The front office on the right was vacant. Further down the hallway, on the right was a Dentist office. At the front of the vacant office were four long thin windows, freshly mulched shrubs, a small grass area, and the asphalt paved parking lot. K-Mart's parking lot ran all the way to the side of the building.

Bill called the number listed and the landlord came right over. Inside the office, there was an office, a place for a receptionist desk, and swinging doors led to a large room.

"What kind of business are you in?" The landlord asked, not wanting to have a conflict with another tenant.

Bill explained his camera business, and asked. "Would you mind if I used the wall facing K-Mart for advertising?"

"Not at all!"

"How much is the rent?"

"Three hundred and fifty a month, first and last months rent in advance."

"Do you require a lease?"

"No!"

Bill wrote a check for seven hundred dollars, and the landlord handed him the keys.

To the left of the office was a small green and white house. Next to it was an Arby's restaurant with a drive-thru window. Directly across from that was Tamaron apartments.

At Tamaron, Bill rented a one bedroom apartment facing the swimming pool on the second floor for two hundred and ninety dollars a month. For thirty dollars a month more, the manager furnished it.

Bill called Debbie. After giving her the addresses for the new store and apartment, he said. "I want you to call and have the gas and electric turned on in both places in my name. Then, call the phone company and set-up appointments to have phones installed. One wall phone in the kitchen at the apartment. At the store, I want three phones at different locations with three incoming lines. Do you know what that means?"

"I think so." Bill explained.

"Three incoming lines will allow you to put one person on hold and answer another call. But it's only one incoming phone number...

"Oh! Okay!"

"Also, call the Bureau of Vital Statistics and order stick-on labels, names and addresses, of new births in Lucas County for the last twelve months."

Tomorrow, in Cleveland Bill would go to see John Stefansky at Capital Finance, then stop by the printers.

Driving down Alexis Road on his way home he noticed a billboard advertising BRONCO BILLY'S - the largest western bar in Ohio, It was behind the Greenwood Mall. On the drive back to Cleveland a thousand thoughts ran through Bill's mind. He was going to need more furniture for the new store, that was for certain. And he would need to hire some help for the Cleveland store. Sales help. That wasn't Lee's strong suit.

## CHAPTER SEVENTEEN
## BRONCO BILLY'S

When Bill arrived back at the store in Cleveland, Debbie was anxiously waiting to fill him in on the days events. "You have two appointments set for tonight. One at six, the other at seven. The utilities are already turned on at the apartment and store in Toledo, they will be transferred into your name. Ohio Bell doesn't offer three lines for a single number, but they do offer a package that includes three incoming numbers. If one line is busy, the incoming call will automatically switch to another line. I ordered that for the store and a regular phone for the apartment. Friday afternoon, at two o'clock, the installer will be at the two and it will take about two hours. As for the apartment, the new number is activated, but you will need to stop by one of their stores and select a phone. If you want a wall phone, there is an additional charge.

"Very good." Bill smiled his approval. "That was the good news. You may not want to hear this. I called the Bureau of Vital Statistics in Columbus, Ohio and ordered the stick-on names and addresses of new births for the past year. Cuyahoga County has a population of 2.8 million and five thousand new births a month. Lucas County has a population of about two hundred and eight thousand with a birth rate of seven hundred a month."

"You're right, I didn't want to hear that!"

"There were around eight thousand new births for the last twelve months. I ordered those!"

"Check the map for outlining counties. We can probably pick up some from there. And, we may have to find another way to generate leads."

That evening, Bill closed on both appointments. But instead of going to the Colonial Boy he went to the house to talk to Lee and Debbie.

"Lee, I'm going to make you the manager of the store in Cleveland. I will be staying at the apartment in Toledo, so Debbie can stay in my room!" Debbie smiled. "Debbie, in the morning I want you to place an ad in the Cleveland Blade for sales help. Lee, if I'm not available, you conduct the interviews. It's strictly commission, One hundred dollars a deal."

* * *

Next, Bill called Bonnie and asked. "How are you doing?"

"Where have you been?" Bonnie asked, a little irritated.

"In Toledo. I'm opening a second store."

"In Toledo?"

"Yes. I have already rented it."

"No, you didn't."

"Yes, I did." Bill chuckled. "But I called to see if you wanted to go out for a bite to eat."

"Now?" Bonnie quizzed.

"No, sometime next year. Of course now!"

"Where are we going?"

"Where would you like to go?"

"I don't care."

"Then why are you asking?"

"Because it makes a difference as to what I wear, dummy."

"I'm dressed casual."

Bill picked Bonnie up and they went to Big Boy's restaurant. They ate, talked, and Bill asked if she wanted to take next Friday off and go to Toledo with him. She did!

The following day Bill stopped by Capital Finance to see John Stefansky, tell him about the new store in Toledo, and ask if he could call someone to help set-up the financing.

"I can't help you with that." John sighed. There's a lot of gossip going on and I'm not sure how much longer I'm going to have a job."

"Why? What's happening?"

"Nothing yet. But if it does, I'll be sure to let you know."

"I appreciate that." Bill said, and shook his friend's hand.

* * *

The t-tops were off. Bonnie's hair was blowing in the wind and it was a beautiful day. She smiled and said. "I went to college in Bowling Green, then asked. "How far is Toledo?"

"It's about ninety miles." Bill pressed down on the accelerator and asked. "Do you want to see how fast we can get there?"

"No!" Bonnie shouted. Bill laughed, and slowed down.

The State Troopers were out in force. They passed two sitting in the median clocking vehicles with hand held radar guns.

The sky looked like little white cotton balls against a baby blue background. A flock of birds, in formation, flew overhead. Bill wasn't much of an outdoorsman, he had no clue as to what kind of birds they were. Bonnie didn't know either.

"Did you know that not all birds migrate?" Bonnie asked.

"No, but I never gave it much thought."

In Toledo, Bill found a printer on Laskey Avenue near Secor. He ordered cards to be mailed out, business cards, and stationary. Then, they went to the store and waited for the installer. There were no chairs in the store, so after showing the installer where he wanted the phones, he drove through Arby's drive-thru and they sat in the car in the parking lot at the store and ate lunch. Bill pointed to the apartments across the street, and said. "The apartment that I rented is right over there!"

The installed phones had clear buttons that flashed when someone called, and stayed lit-up when someone was placed on hold. If one line was busy, the call would automatically transfer to the next available line. The secretary could answer the phone, place the caller and hold, then buzz Bill's office which meant the call was for him. The nearest Ohio Bell phone center was in the Southwyck Mall. Bill rented an inexpensive wall phone for the kitchen.

When they stopped by the apartment, the furniture was there. "That's got to be the ugliest sofa that I've ever seen." Bill said, sitting down. It was a crappy brown with a wooden frame and three square cushions across the back and bottom.

"I've seen worse." Bonnie chimed in.

The bed was only a twin, but it was comfortable. There was a end table, a lamp, and a five drawer dresser.

The next stop was K-Mart. Bill grabbed a shopping cart. He knew exactly what he needed. Toilet paper, soap, towels, face clothes, linens, two soft pillows, and a blanket.

That evening they had dinner and drinks at Ahmed's Steak House. They spent the night at the apartment, but were on the road to Cleveland by eight o'clock in the morning. Bill only had the weekend to get the store together, and he a lot of work ahead of him.

Bonnie read the billboard aloud. "Bronco Billy's, the largest western bar in Ohio. Behind the Greenwood Mall."

"The Greenwood Mall is on the left about a mile from here. It's before Interstate 75, our exit. I haven't been there yet."

"How can you miss the largest country western bar in Ohio?" Bonnie smiled.

\* \* \*

After dropping Bonnie at her apartment, he drove downtown to the new and used Office Supply store. He bought a used yellow metal desk with an imitation wood grain top, an office chair, and two brown cushioned chairs for customers. He bought a two-piece white metal secretarial desk with an imitation wood grain top, a secretary chair, and a used IBM typewriter for the receptionist.

Then, he called Lee at the house and said. "Meet me at the store."

"Give me twenty minutes." Lee replied. If there was one person Bill could depend on, it was Lee. He never asked why, he was just dependable. Bill picked Lee up, drove to U-Haul and rented a truck for the weekend. He drove to the Office Supply store, loaded the furniture he had purchased earlier, then stopped at Best Products in Willowick and purchased eight hundred dollars in merchandise to stock the Toledo store. Then, he stopped at Modern Camera and asked if they had any extra display merchandise, such as posters or large Kodak film boxes. The last stop was at B & H

Camera. Bill took ten Bell & Howell camera's and projectors from stock.

In the basement of the store, he found a row of four metal seats on a metal frame. It needed to be reupholstered. Bill also loaded that onto the truck.

Monday morning he intended go to Capital Finance Company in Toledo, introduce himself, pick-up contracts and delivery slips and he would be in business. Lee would deliver the two pending contracts written at the Cleveland store to John with delivery slips, pick up the checks, and deposit those into the business account at Dollar bank. At least, that was his plan. Jenny stayed at the house with the kids, while Lee and Debbie went with Bill to Toledo. They were both anxious to see the new store, and apartment. After unloading the truck at the store, they stopped by the apartment. Lee opened the patio door, stood on the small balcony admiring the swimming pool and clubhouse, grinned, and offered. "Are you sure that you don't want to stay in Cleveland?"

They drove around Toledo checking out the area. There was a small bar catty-corner to Tamaron apartments, the sign read, RODEO BAR. As they pulled into the graveled lot, there were only two other vehicles. Debbie made a beeline to the jukebox while Bill ordered drinks and chesseburgers.

"Want to play a game of pool?" Bill asked Lee, noticing the table and rack of cue sticks.

"You rack, I'll break." Lee said, accepting the challenge.

There was only one customer in the bar, an elderly man sitting on a barstool at the far end of the counter talking with the barmaid. He was wearing blue jeans, a dusty cowboy hat, a blue plaid shirt with suspenders, and well worn cowboy boots. His mustache curled at both ends and he didn't talk like most people, he growled. Bill's first impression was he wasn't the type of man someone would want trouble with. It wasn't until he stood up and walked to the men's room that Bill noticed his right arm was amputated and he limped badly, even with a cane.

The barmaid, an attractive brunette in her early thirties, introduced herself as, Joyce. She was very friendly and easy on the eyes. Joyce was wearing jeans, with white top tied in a knot exposing her well tanned flat stomach.

Bill won the game, then asked Debbie if she wanted to play a game with Lee. He wanted to take the opportunity to talk with Joyce. His first question was. "How far does Alexis Road go?"

"I'm not sure. But I do know that it runs from Interstate 75 fifteen miles down Alexis Road, crosses over Highway 23, and goes through the City of Sylvania. I'm not sure where it ends?" Joyce answered.

"I've seen a billboard advertising Bronco Billy's. Have you been there?"

"Yes! It's behind the Greenwood Mall. The inside is huge but it doesn't open until after 5 o'clock. There's a Cab of a Semi truck sticking out of a wall. That's where the DJ spins records. There's a stage, a live band, and dancing. In the rear, there's a mechanical bull."

"A mechanical bull?" Bill repeated.

"A big black one!" Joyce giggled.

"Have you tried to ride it?"

"Twice! I got bucked off both times. There's ten speeds. The first is amateur. I've never made it beyond that." Joyce sighed her disappointment.

"Where are all of your customers?" "We get a crowd at lunch time. Workers from GM, Jeep, and the Dana corporation. It picks up again after six o' clock. On the weekends, unless you come early you won't be able to find a parking space. There's live entertainment, a Country band. "

That evening Bill paid the two dollar cover charge at the door for himself, Lee, and Debbie to enter Bronco Billy's. On their right was a Cab of a Semi that appeared to be driving through a white cinder block wall. The Cab was complete with a windshield, doors, and a steering wheel. The interior had been gutted and replaced with high tech stereo equipment. Directly below the Cab was a stage for the band. In front of the stage, there was a dance floor. In the center of the room there was an enormous horseshoe bar thirty feet wide and a three hundred feet around with barstools all of the way around it. The overhead lighting was inverted tin wash tubs spaced ten feet apart. Tables and booths were spread around the room. In the rear of the bar there was a western apparel store on one side, and a mechanical bull on the other. The black bull was fenced in with thick gray mats on the floor to comfort the riders falling from grace.

"I'll pay if you will ride it!" Bill offered Debbie.

"I'm not getting on that thing." She frowned at the suggestion.

Bill noticed there was no one taking photos of the customers riding the bull. There was nothing for the customer to take home to show to their friends, or to remember their good time. And above the stage there was a slide projector.

When the house band took the stage the DJ spun the record, Roll on Eighteen Wheeler, and no one could tell where the record stopped and the band took over. It was Bronco Billy's theme song!

Bill soon learned there were nine co-owners. A guy by the name of Billy Hotelie had brought them together in a joint venture. He also owned a restaurant in Chicago that he named after himself, "Billy's". And Billy was bellied up to the bar when Bill approached him.

"I noticed that you don't have anyone taking photos of customers riding the mechanical bull."

Billy grinned, then replied. "If I had my way, that damn thing wouldn't be in here. I sell liquor!"

"My name is Bill Burns". Bill introduced himself. "I'm new to the area and I'm opening a camera shop in front of K-Mart. Would you be interested in our taking photos, if a percentage of the profit went to Bronco Billy's?"

"Put it on paper. Give me something to look at. I'm a visual kind of guy." Billy chuckled. He took a sip from his drink, then chewed on a cube of ice.

Billy stood six feet and weighed a solid two hundred pounds. He had dark hair and brown eyes. His slacks were tailored, his shirts imported, and he wore a thick gold chain around his neck with a Saint Christopher medallion. On his left wrist, he wore an expensive gold watch. Everything about Billy presented a picture of success.

"Nice meeting you." Bill smiled, then added an afterthought. "I'll get back with you as soon as I put something together."

## CHAPTER EIGHTEEN
## BARKEY'S OF AMERICA

Sunday morning Bill, Lee, and Debbie returned to the house in Cleveland. Jenny was in the kitchen preparing sandwiches for the kids for lunch.

"How was your trip?" She asked Debbie, smiling.

"It was okay. The new store is nice, but I like the one in Cleveland better."

Early Monday morning, Bill returned the U-Haul truck, then drove to Modern Camera. The old man was outside sweeping the sidewalk when the white Trans-Am parked at the curb. As Bill opened. the car door, he grinned and said." I thought you drove a silver car!"

"I do, sometimes." Bill explained. "I have a 1979 silver Cadillac El Dorado and this 1981 white Trans-Am."

"That's pretty sporty looking."

"It's the Special Edition, the Indy Pace car."

"Aw, I think I would prefer the comfort."

"Are you open for business yet?"

"Sure, sure. What can I do for you?" He asked, sweeping the trash into one pile.

"I need a camera to take photos of people riding a mechanical bull. An instant photo! Any suggestions?"

"Polaroid makes a camera with a interchangeable wide angle lens. It has a fast shutter speed, and you will need that! Wholesale it will cost five hundred dollars, and I don't have one in stock."

"Does it take the standard size film?"

"I'm pretty sure that it does."

"How long will it take for you to get one?"

"A week to ten days."

"Order it!" Bill smiled. Debbie was sitting behind her desk sipping a cup of coffee and Lee was playing the pin ball machine when Bill walked in. As Lee's fingers touched buttons on both sides of the machine, the flippers sprang to life sending the steel ball bouncing. Ding, ding, ding. Then, there was a brief silence and Lee shouted. "Shit!" as the word TILT appeared on the screen at the top.

"I'm fine with your playing the game, but use some discretion. If Debbie is on the phone, or Mark has a client in his office don't play the game."

"You need to stop by the Post Office today and pick up the mailers." Debbie told Bill. When customers mailed film in to be developed it was important that Debbie process and remail the film to the 3M Company. Inside the prepaid mailing envelope was the customers name and address. 3M mailed the developed film directly to the customer.

"Get John at Capital Finance on the phone. Tell him that if he's free for lunch that I'm buying."

As Bill walked through the doors to Mark's office, Cindy and baby Jesse weren't there. Mark said that wasn't a bad thing and that he wished he had a bed in his office so he could get some sleep.

"How is everything going with the store in Toledo?" Mark inquired.

"So far, so good. Did Lee or Debbie tell you about Bronco Billy's?"

"No, they did not."

"It's the largest western bar in Ohio and they have a mechanical bull. I'm hoping that B & H Camera will soon be taking photos of customers riding the bull. I would like to use that to promote the store."

"Sounds good!" Mark smiled.

"How's your business?" Bill asked Mark.

"Some weeks are better than others. It's picking up."

Debbie interrupted. "John said to pick him up at noon, and for you not to forget your wallet."

Bill chuckled. At noon, he picked John up driving the Trans-Am with the tops off.

"Have you ever been to the Lamp Light?" Bill asked.

"I can't say that I have."

"It's a small Irish Pub just down the street. They serve good food."

When they walked through the front door, Gary was standing behind the bar wiping the counter clean with a rag.

"How have you been?" Bill asked Gary with a smile.

"Good! And you?" Gary asked.

"Busy!" "Did you and your brother ever get that spa thing together? What was it called?"

"Octopool. No, we never obtained the financing."

"Sorry to hear about that. It sounded like a great idea."

"Gary, this is my friend, John."

"Pleased to meet you."

"I've been telling John what a great chef you are. And, we are here for lunch."

"And you would like a greasy what?" Gary chuckled.

"I'll have a BLT with fries. You can't mess that up!" Bill smiled.

"Double that order." John added.

"Would you like to sit at the counter, or would you prefer a booth?" Bill gave John the option.

"Let's sit at a booth. I have some things to discuss."

"Good news?" Bill asked, with raised eyebrows.

"I'm not sure." As they seated themselves, one across from the other. John continued. "I heard through the grapevine that Barkley's of America may be buying Capital Finance Company."

"How would that affect me?"

"I honestly don't know. If it happens, I may not have a job."

"What would you do?" Bill asked.

"I don't have a back-up plan. I never thought that I would need one!"

"Remember this. You were looking for a job when you found that one."

On the drive back to the office, Bill stopped by the Post Office and picked up mailers of film customers had mailed in. The flap of each envelope reminds the customer to include ninety cents for postage and handling. Most frequently the customer would simply put One dollar inside the envelope. While others would include a personal check. Debbie smiled when Bill walked into the store carrying the gray bag. Debbie logged the mailers into a book, then transferred the film to the prepaid mailer. The customers name was written on a label and 3M used that label for the return address.

"Lee just went to lunch." Debbie volunteered. Within an hour Bill was on his way back to Toledo. The Trans Am was on cruise control, the wind was whistling through the car, and the stereo was booming.

It was a gorgeous day and he was alone with his thoughts. He thought of his childhood, and smiled. At five, his family lived in Jacksonville Beach, Florida. His father was the manager of a Firestone Tire Store. One evening, he came home with a large cardboard box full of seeds that he had taken from a display rack at work, the company was throwing them into the garbage. His father divided the seeds equally between him, his older brother, and younger sister. There was a variety of seeds - flowers, vegetables, and shrubbery. With the help of her mother, his sister planted a garden. His brother took his seeds door to door selling them at half price. That night Bill went for a ride with his father to the hardware store. He purchased a hammer and nails. Bill noticed the hardware store sold the same identical seeds. So, he took the bag from his fathers purchase, put his seeds inside the bag, and returned them to the hardware the following day for a full refund.

When he was five, he walked up and down the aisles of the IGA grocery store until he found a woman shopper by herself. With a bag of candy in one hand and a few coins in the other he would ask. "Do I have enough money to buy this?"

"No honey, you don't."

"It's my mother's birthday, and I've been saving." He would cry, tears streaming from both eyes.

"Oh! You poor boy. Here you go," and they would fork over the rest of the money, every time. Women were such suckers. That is, until he ran up to the same one twice. She chased him out of the store, ending his career.

Once a year, his father took his children to the doctor for a yearly flu shot. As Bill, his brother, and sister were seated waiting, the doctor stepped into the room, and asked. "Who's first?"

Bill, his brother and sister looked at each other to see if anyone was going to volunteer. After a minute of silence, Bill said. "Well, Dad. You always told me ladies before gentlemen."

* * *

In Toldeo, before going to the new store, Bill stopped at K-Mart and purchased a ream of typing paper, pens and pencils, a desk calendar, an appointment book, and two plastic folder with inserts. Stepping into the hallway of the store the cool air hit him squarely in the face. It felt refreshing! Once inside the office, he went through magazines, cutting out pictures, preparing two presentation booklets. One presentation book would be for the store customers as examples of what they might use a camera for. The other presentation book would be presented to Billy Hotelie at Bronco Billy's. It would be his written proposal!

Bill met Brad Bernhagen, an unemployed carpenter, at Bronco Billy's. He asked Brad if he could build a large glass cabinet.

"No problem!" He replied, with confidence. Brad agreed to meet Bill at the store at noon the following day. Three girls were seated at a small round table. Bill introduced himself offering to buy them a drink. From left to right, they introduced themselves. Cindy Meyers, Beth Whitson, and Sharon Johnson. Sharon was married. Cindy had a boyfriend and worked at Kroger's. And Beth was a single mother of one.

When Billy Hotelie walked into the bar, Bill excused himself.

He walked up to Billy, and asked. "Can I buy you a drink?"

"Sure." Billy chuckled. "But I'm not going home with you!"

Bill laughed heartily. "I'm working on the camera deal and I should have something for you in the next couple of days."

"Let me know when you do!"

# CHAPTER NINETEEN
# DOUBLE TROUBLE

The following day at noon Brad went to the store. Bill walked him through the swinging doors to the back room and explained what he wanted. A four foot cabinet with sliding doors fifteen feet long. On top of that a display cabinet with sliding glass doors and glass shelves five feet high.

"I can build it here, stain it, and have the glass cut. Working nights, I can build it in three days at a cost of approximately seven hundred dollars."

"When can you start?"

"Now!" Brad smiled.

"Do you know a painter? I'm looking for someone who can paint a mural on the side of the building. I want a camera, projector, and the words FREE IF YOU DO YOUR FILM DEVELOPING WITH US, with the businesses name and phone number."

Brad made a phone call. Twenty minutes later he introduced Bill to his friend, Chet. Chet looked at the wall as a huge canvas. First, he would paint the entire wall white. His fee would be four hundred dollars. Bill quickly agreed.

\* \* \*

Bill ran into a glitch. There was no Capital Finance Company in Toledo. He called John in Toledo. John explained that Bill could write the contracts through his branch. The catch twenty-two was the contract would need to be called in, approved, and he would need the contract with a delivery slip before he could issue a check, which meant a lot of driving back and forth between Toledo and Cleveland for Bill. But there was no other option!

\* \* \*

Bronco Billy's was packed when Bill arrived at eight o'clock and the band wouldn't take the stage for another hour. Through the windshield of the Cab of the Semi he noticed the DJ wasn't alone, two girls were with him. He spotted Billy Hotelie standing bellied up to the bar, walked over to him, and asked. "Have you got a minute?"

Billy turned his head slightly to his right, and said. "What's up?"

Bill opened a folder, announcing. "I have something for you. He explained in more detail. "This is the cost of the equipment, the cost for the film, and I'm estimating that thirty photos will be sold every night with One dollar per photo to be paid to Bronco Billy's."

Somewhat impressed, Billy raised his eyebrows.

Bill continued. "And with your permission, I would like to build a western scene for couples to take photos. All that would require is a ten by ten feet area against the wall next to mechanical bull."

"How much is that going to cost?"

"I'll bear the expense to build it." Bill replied.

"How much is it going to cost the customer for a photo?"

"Three dollars."

"I'm not concerned with the bar making any money. I sell liquor! Sell the photos for two dollars, and you've got a deal."

Two weeks later, Bill bought a color TV and a video recorder for the store in Toledo. On nights when he was bored, he would rent movies.

It took three days to build the camera stand inside Bronco Billy's. Bill used railroad ties at the bottom, fenced in the area to match the wooden fence where the mechanical bull was housed, filled the inside with sand, and created the illusion of cactus' made from plaster against the wall. Chet painted a sunset on the wall and the cactus' green. Everyone was impressed, including Billy. And he wasn't easily impressed.

Bill had his first three appointments. He called the contracts in to John at Capital Finance in Cleveland. Two were approved, one wasn't. Bill had expected that. The guy rejected didn't have very much of a credit history and had only been at his job for a year.

The store in Toledo was coming along better than Bill had anticipated. Chet had painted the mural. In the upper left corner he painted a projector. In the right, a 35 millimeter camera. He painted the name B & H Camera and the phone number in black, bordered in red. It was an eye catcher! People driving up and down Alexis Road or shoppers at K-Mart were sure to be attracted to the billboard on the side of the building.

Friday, Bill drove to Toledo. As he walked through the front door of the store, Debbie said. John from Modern Camera called. Whatever he ordered for you is there."

"That's good. How has business been?"

"Lee hired two sales people. Marty is in his forties. His last job was selling shoes. Debbie is probably in her early thirties. She's nice, lives within walking distance, isn't married, and has three kids. This week I scheduled nine appointments. Two were no shows. One rescheduled. And, there were no sales."

"None?" Bill said, shaking his head in disgust.

"Sorry!" Debbie smiled half-heartedly.

"Where's Lee?"

"He just went to the Post Office."

"Do you have any appointments scheduled for Monday night?"

"Three, the first one at five-thirty."

"I'll be here! I need for someone to help me understand why no contracts are being written."

Mark walked through the hallway into the store, and said. "I thought I heard you. How are things going at the new store?"

"Better than they are here!" Bill replied.

"Have you ridden that mechanical bull yet?" Mark grinned.

"No! I'm waiting for Debbie to show me how." Bill chuckled.

Debbie giggled, and said. "That's going to be a long wait."

Bill challenged Mark to a game of pinball, and he quickly accepted suggesting. "Let's let Debbie play. The loser has to wash all of the windows in the store and office - inside, and out."

Bill chuckled. "Why would I make a bet like that when I can just tell her to do it."

"No, you can't!" Debbie snapped. "I vacuum and pick up after you guys every day, all day."

Bill and Mark laughed. No wager was made. But, much to their dismay, Debbie won the game. Mark came in last.

"I see what you've been doing when I'm not here." Bill smiled at Debbie. He left the store, picked up the Polaroid camera and wide angle lens from Modern Camera, then drove to Capital Finance to give John his contracts and delivery slips, and collect his checks.

"Let's go to lunch, John. Where would you like to go?"

"Let's go to the Lamp Light."

They sat in the same booth, ordered the same sandwiches, but this time John ordered a Rum and Coca-Cola with his lunch.

"How have things been going?" Bill inquired.

"Not so good. For the last week I have had auditors in my office going through the files, one by one."

"You haven't done anything illegal, have you?"

"Of course not!"

"Are you still worried about losing your job?"

"Not at this point. Barkley's of America is buying Capital Finance Company, but they announced they have no intentions of letting any of the staff go."

"Then, what's the problem?"

John frowned. "I don't know how to tell you this." "Tell me what?" Bill pushed for more information. "I cannot accept any more contracts written from the Toledo store."

"Why?" "I wasn't given a reason. I was simply told point blank that I couldn't do it."

"What about the Cleveland store?" "The only store addressed, and they 'specifically' addressed was the Toledo store."

"John, you have been a very good friend. I understand that business is business and sometimes the two don't mix well. I'm fine with this! I will find another finance company in Toledo. On the bright side, that will stop me from having to drive back and forth every Friday." Bill smiled.

* * *

When Bill walked through the door of Bronco Billy's that night he was waived through, there would be no cover charge for him or his guests. Billy was standing bellied up to the bar sipping a drink and chewing cubed ice. Bill walked up, stood beside him, and announced. "The camera stand will be open for business next weekend. I just picked up the Polariod camera and wide angle lens. The damn camera cost five hundred dollars!"

"Stop crying. You're breaking my heart." Billy chuckled.

"I don't suppose that you would care to reimburse me?" Bill said with a grin.

"Not in this lifetime!" Billy sipped his drink. He motioned to the head barmaid, Sheila. When she walked over, Billy said, "Give Bill a drink and put it on my tab."

"Tab?" Bill repeated with a snicker, then asked, "What do I need to do to be able to run a tab?"

Bill ordered a seven and seven in a tall glass. As Sheila placed the drink in front of him, Billy added. "And run a tab for Bill."

Cindy, Beth, and Sharon were seated at the table where he had met them. Bill pointed, and said. "Sheila, give those three girls a drink and put it on my tab."

Billy Hotelie almost spit his drink all over himself. "Boy, that was quick! Don't forget to pay your tab at the end of the month."

"No problem." Bill replied, then grinned and said. "Shella, give Billy a drink on me too!"

Twenty minutes later, Bill walked over to the girls table. Sharon smiled and said. "I saw the mural on the side of the building. It's nice."

"Whose idea was it to put the cactus on the wall?" Beth asked.

"It was my idea. Do you like it?"

"Yes!" Beth smiled, adding. "It looks three dimensional."

"When are you going to start taking photos?" Cindy asked.

"Next week if I can find someone to hire."

"I know someone who is looking for work and they're dependable." Beth offered.

"Tell them to give me a call." Bill smiled.

"I'll call and ask him to come down now." Beth stood up, left the table and made a phone call. Twenty minutes later, she introduced Bill to Dan Ruffing. Dan was five eleven, stocky, with shoulder length brown hair and brown eyes. He was wearing blue jeans, a nice shirt, and a black three quarter length leather jacket. He spoke well, and presented himself even better.

"Do you have any experience?" Bill asked.

"Not really. I have a 35 millimeter camera and I think I take pretty good photos."

"This is pretty simple. It's a Polaroid camera with a wide angle lens. My main objection is to promote my business."

"What business is that?" Dan inquired.

"I own a camera store in Cleveland. A month ago I opened a second store on Alexis Road in front of K-Mart."

"Is that your mural on the wall?"

"That's me!" Bill smiled, happy the mural was being noticed.

"Look! This is what I'm willing to do. I have made a good size investment between the camera equipment and camera stand. But I want you to think of this as your business. I'll start you out. From there, you buy the film, take the photos, and charge the customer two dollars per photo. The profit will be your salary. My only requirement is that you are here when you're supposed to be - from six o' clock until closing. Would that proposition be of interest?"

"Sounds more than fair to me. When do I start?"

"Next Friday night. But come by the store tomorrow afternoon and I will get you set up."

"How's two o'clock?"

"Sounds good." Bill smiled.

Dan showed up on time, and Bill gave him the camera equipment along with the manual so he could familiarize himself with the camera. He provided Dan with four rolls of Polaroid film. After that, he would need to purchase film.

* * *

Monday morning Bill went to Fair Financing on Lasky Road. He introduced himself to the manager, set up financing, and left the office with contracts and delivery receipts in hand. The downside was, unlike John at Capital Finance Company in Cleveland, the manager wasn't authorized to give instant approval unless the contract was written in his office. This meant there would be a twenty-four to seventy-two hour waiting period for approval. in Bill's thoughts, this sucked. But there was no other option.

* * *

Friday Bill drove to the Cleveland store to meet Lee's sales staff. Marty was a short Italian with black hair. He was clean and neat, but lacking in personality. Debbie had auburn hair that fell to her shoulders. She was cute, but again no personality. As Marty gave the presentation, Bill observed. Marty turned the pages of the presentation book going through the motion of telling the potential customer of what they might use a camera for - birthdays, weddings, special events. Then, he played with the camera and asked if they would be interested in buying into the program.

"See, I told you it's not free!" The wife snapped.

"No, we're not interested!" The husband said. The couple stood up and were on their way out the door when Bill stepped from the back office. He introduced himself as the owner, shook the husband's hand, and asked for a few minutes of their time. The husband looked at his wife as she shrugged her shoulders. The couple sat back down.

"This equipment is absolutely FREE. As a matter of fact, I will also include a carrying case, screen, and your first roll of film. What I want in return is your developing business. You are free to purchase your film anywhere!"

"You would develop your film with us, wouldn't you?" Bill asked, smiling.

"Yes, but probably not 300 rolls." The wife answered.

"That does sound like an awful lot. How old is your baby?"

"Six months this Thursday." The wife proudly announced.

"Well, do you think that you would film fifteen hours of your baby's life?"

"Of course!"

"Well, each roll last three minutes and twenty seconds. It takes ten rolls to make a thirty minute movie. Twenty rolls for one hour. Do the math, that is three hundred rolls."

"It is, isn't it." The wife agreed looking to her husband for his thoughts.

"We offer a lifetime in which for you to develop the film. If you move, you can still use the mailers. If the price of developing goes up, that doesn't affect you because you prepaid the cost of the processing."

The husband and wife left the office with the camera package and were happy customers.

Twice, customers were walking out after Marty's presentation and Bill brought back and closed the deal.

"Lee, we've got to talk later. Right now I've got to get on the road. It's an hour and a-half drive back to Toledo."

The bed in the apartment was a welcoming sight. Sleep came quickly.

In the morning when Bill walked into the showroom of his store in Toledo, he admired the cabinets that Brad built. They were beautiful, but bare.

Wednesday Debbie called. She had scheduled nine appointments, none closed. "The store needs you, Bill."

"Schedule appointments for Friday, beginning at three. I don't care how late they run. I'll be there!" Bill promised.

Friday afternoon Bill drove to Cleveland and closed four package deals.

After closing the store, he took Debbie with him to Best Products and purchased thirty-eight hundred dollars in merchandise to fill the cabinet in the store in Toledo. Then, he treated her to a steak dinner at Ponderosa. He dropped Debbie at the house and drove back to Toledo.

Saturday night, after closing Bronco Billy's Bill went to breakfast with Beth, Sharon, Cindy, and Dan. Then, he took Beth to the store and they laid on the floor watching video's until the wee hours of the morning. The following day, she introduced Bill to her parents and unruly son, Danny. He was five, and cursed like a drunken sailor. The house was a red brick split level with a two-car attached garage on Vistamar Drive in Shoreland.

Beth was short with brown hair, brown eyes. A "daddy's little girl" spoiled from birth. Whatever she wanted, she got. George had recently bought her a restored 1969 red Camaro Super Sport with a black vinyl top.

Beth's father, George, was short, slightly overweight, and balding. But he combed his hair to the side to cover his balding. Her mother, Joyce O' 'Rourke Whitson was the Matriarch of the family. She was well rounded, bubbly, and a joy to be around. To sum her up, she was "a lady".

George was talented. At work, he made renderings. At home, he enjoyed painting in his upstairs studio. His paintings were thoughtfully hung about the house.

"Do you want to go to the Kentucky Derby with me next weekend?" Beth invited Bill.

"Sounds like fun." He smiled.

* * *

Monday morning Debbie called Bill at the store in Toledo in a panic. "When Lee went to pick up the checks at Capital Finance, the checks weren't issued. There's a problem and John says that he needs to speak with you as soon as possible."

Bill called John right away. "Barkley's of America. How may I help you?"

"Is John Stefansky in, please."

"He's on another line, may I ask whose calling?"

"Bill Burns. And, I'll hold."

A few minutes later, John came on the line. "Hello, Bill. I'm afraid that I've got some bad news for you? Barkley's is eliminating some businesses and B & H Camera is one of those."

"Why?" Bill asked, somewhat caught offguard.

"There is a law that I was unfamiliar with, Holder in Due Course. What that means is that if you were to go out of business, Barkley's of America would have to fulfill the conditions of the contract or the contract would become null and void. In other words, they would have to develop the 300 rolls of film."

"I don't put the developing of film on the contract. The loan is secured by the camera and projector." Bill countered.

"It doesn't matter. Underwritten it's still 'a part' of the contract. Barkley's of America instructed me to tell you that they don't want to be partners with you anymore."

"I'll have to close the business. Are they willing to write off two hundred thousand dollars in contracts?"

"I'm sorry, Bill. They've made their decision."

"Well, what about the four approved contracts?"

"I'm sorry, Bill. I truly am."

"I've written checks that I can't cover!"

"I wish there was something that I could do. Believe me, I didn't want to have to be the one to have to tell you this."

"Holy shit!" Bill said, more to himself.

## CHAPTER TWENTY
## KENTUCKY DERBY

Bill drove to the house in Cleveland to meet with Lee, Jenny, and Debbie.

"Barkley's of America bought Capital Finance Company and they've canceled the financing for the store in Cleveland. Because of that, I'm going to have to close the store. I don't know how, but I will pay another months rent on the house. By then, you're going to have to find a place of your own. In the morning I am going to rent a U-Haul truck and Lee and I will move everything from the Cleveland store to Toledo. Debbie, the only option that I can offer you is to live at the apartment and work at the Toledo store. Unless someone has a better plan, that's all I can do."

"I'll go to Toledo!" Debbie quickly made her decision.

After moving everything in the store to Toledo, Lee drove the U-Haul back to Cleveland.

Debbie immediately starting unpacking, putting her things away, and cleaning the apartment.

* * *

Saturday morning. Bill and Beth were on their way to the Kentucky Derby. Bill was driving her fire engine red Camaro looking down the black racing stripe on the hood. They were heading South on Interstate 75 just outside of Bowling Green when a State Trooper on the opposite side of the highway hit his brakes, cut across the median, turned on his overhead lights, and pulled the Camaro over.

"May I see your driver's license, registration, and proof of insurance?" The officer asked, standing at the driver window.

"May I ask why you pulled us over officer?" Bill asked politely.

"No front license plate!"

Beth grinned, and said. "I've never had a problem before." The Trooper walked to his car, returning a few minutes later.

"Mr. Burns, step out of the car, please." Bill complied, wondering what the problem was. But before he asked, the officer said. "Mr. Burns, there is a warrant for your arrest out of Cleveland, Ohio."

"For what?" Bill asked, at a loss for reasoning.

"I don't know. I was instructed to arrest you! Face the car, and put your hands behind your back." In seconds Bill was handcuffed, placed in the back seat of the Trooper's car, and taken to the State Trooper station in Bowling Green. He was fingerprinted, his photo taken, and placed in a holding cell for the night. The next morning, Bill appeared before a magistrate in Bowling Green. To his surprise, Beth was there. Bond was set at five hundred dollars.

"What's the charge for? And, what do you want me to do?"

"A check written to Best Products in Willowyck, Ohio bounced. It was to be covered by four contracts that were approved. Without warning, my financing was canceled and the contracts voided."

"It's just a bounced check?" Beth repeated.

"Yes! You should go home. But I appreciate your coming." Bill used his one phone call to call Ed, one of three brothers who were among the nine co-owners in Bronco Billy's. Ed loaned money, and twice Bill had borrowed money and repaid Ed when he promised. Forty-five minutes later Ed arrived at the jail and posted Bill's bail. When he was released, Ed gave him a ride back to his apartment. Bill was wearing a short sleeve shirt and jeans. And it was the first time anyone from Bronco Billy's had seen his tattoos. On Bill's left arm he had a colorful Peacock that extended from his elbow down to his wrist. Above the elbow, a huge Eagle in flight. On his lower right arm there was a rose with a butterfly. Above his elbow, a hippie sitting on top of a mushroom smoking a water pipe. Bill tried to keep his tattoos hidden, to the extent that he wore his watch on his left wrist.

Bill noticed Ed looking at his tattoos, but he said nothing. They were prison tattoos that were done by another prisoner when he was at McNeil Island but at least they looked professional.

"Have you got a minute?" Bill broke the silence. "I'd like to show you my store."

"Sure." Ed was very impressed. The store was stocked to the brim with the holdings of the Cleveland store.

\* \* \*

Monday morning Bill called Mark, and said. "I've got a problem. "

"What this time, Billy Boy. I see you've closed the store in Cleveland."

"I didn't have a choice. Barkley's of America bought Capital Finance Company and they canceled my customer financing because of a law, Holder in Due Course."

"Holder what?"

"I'll explain that later. Yesterday I was in route to the Kentucky Derby when a State Trooper pulled over the Camaro that I was driving because it didn't have a front license plate."

"That's not a huge problem." Mark chuckled.

"I spent the night in jail!"

"For not having a front license plate?"

"No! I went to jail because there was a warrant for my arrest for a bounced check to Best Products in Willowyck, Ohio. The check is for $3800. I had counted on four approved contracts. Without notice, my financing was cut and Barkley's refused to honor those approvals. Best Products immediately turned the check over to the prosecutor's office."

"Don't pay it!" Mark insisted. "If you pay it, then we have no bargaining power. When is your court date?"

"Next Wednesday."

"Luckily for you my schedule is free. Bring the cash with you to pay the check."

"I'll pick you up at your office at nine o'clock." Bill promised.

"And you're buying lunch!" Mark chuckled. George, Beth's father, offered to loan Bill the money to pay off the bounced check. Bill graciously accepted his kind gesture.

\* \* \*

"The State of Ohio verses William Daniel Burns." The clerk called.

Bill and Mark stood, walked to the defendants table, and remained standing.

"Your honor, my name is Mark Knevel K-n-e-v-e-1, counsel for the defendant."

"What do we have here?" the judge asked, shuffling through papers.

The young prosecutor waived Bill's extensive criminal history in the air, which included a conviction for bank robbery. "Your honor, the defendant has traded his gun for a pen! And, I'm not clear on who he is today. Burns, or Hooker?"

Mark grinned, looked at Bill, and asked. "Is there something you haven't told me? This might be a good time. I hate surprises!"

"The Witness Protection Program changed my name to Burns." Bill admitted. The judge, somewhat amused, chuckled.

Bill's worst fear had just happened. Burns and Hooker had become synonymous.

Mark explained that a business check written to Best Products in good faith had bounced. Had anyone contacted his client, he would have rushed right over to pay the check. It bounced because four approved contracts were not honored by Barkley's of America. Bill paid the check, and the charge was dismissed. But, the damage was done! Burns and Hooker were now synonymous with his criminal history.

As Bill and Mark walked from the courthouse, mark grabbed his sunglasses and covered his eyes to shield them from the glaring sun, then said. "You owe me lunch."

"That I do." Bill smiled. "McDonald's is right around the corner."

"Not exactly what I had in mind, but I will settle for Ponderosa Steak House, the closest one is in Parma."

"Works for me."

Fifteen minutes later they were inside the restaurant. Mark ordered a T-bone medium well while Bill ordered the larger steak, the Porterhouse.

"For some reason, I just never thought of you as a criminal."

"I never planned to be one!" Bill grinned.

"Do you mind if I ask what landed you in the witness protection program?"

"I'm not sure where to begin."

"Try from the beginning." Mark suggested.

"I was born in Lakeland, Florida. When I was five my family moved to Baltimore, Maryland. I was twelve when my parents divorced. My elder brother and younger sister chose to live with my mother. I chose my father. When I was fourteen my father remarried. At fifteen my step mother gave my father an ultimatum, either I leave or she would. I quit school, and left home.

"At twenty, I was married with two daughters, the youngest crying for milk. I had no money, no job, and no one to turn to for help. I committed a burglary and got caught. I gave a statement and I was released on a personal recognize bond. The police made a 'game' of it by telling me they wore uniforms and rode around in marked cars. They asked 'what does a criminal look like?' I bought a yellow panel truck, wrote THIEF WAGON in bold black letters across the back and sides. Then I installed a police scanner. Night after night I heard the dispatcher announce a yellow panel truck leaving scene. The newspapers reported that I was more notorious than Robin Hood in Sherwood Forest."

Mark chucked, took a bite of his steak, and motioned with his fork for Bill to continue.

"December 13, 1968 – Friday the thirteenth, I shot and killed a 36 year old ex prize boxer, Johnny Campbell. The newspapers wrote SLAYING OF SUB SHOP OWNER LINKED TO LOVE TRIANGLE and MAN TRIES TO SEE EX-GIRLFRIEND SLAIN AFTER BREAK-IN. I was charged with homicide in Baltimore City and the outlining counties wrote their unsolved burglaries off on me. I met John Brady in the Anne Arundel County jail and Lennard Hall in the Baltimore County jail. Both set precedents in the United States Supreme Court and they were on death row together. Brady versus Maryland. Brady material?"

"Every lawyer knows that case!" Mark grinned.

"John also wrote the book Between Life and Death. Lennard Hall established guidelines on search and seizure."

"Reason to believe and stop and frisk has pretty much overruled that."

"The homicide was ruled justifiable and dismissed. Anne Arundel County had charged me with thirty burglaries. I pled guilty to two and nolo-contendre to six, the rest were dropped. Judge Evans sentenced me to serve eight eight-year consecutive sentences. I said, "your honor, I thought nolo-contendre meant not guilty."

"Ignorance of the law is no defense!" the judge responded.

My mother went to see the commissioner for Anne Arudel County, Jack Evertts. And he told her: "Kat, why didn't you come to me to start with? Your boy never had to go to prison. I put Judge Evans in his office."

"Judge Evans agreed to hold my case sub curie pending the disposition of charges in Baltimore and Talbot County. Baltimore County dropped their burglary charge. In Talbot County I was charged with Storehouse Breaking and Conspiracy along with codefendant Butch Geohegian. I agreed to plead guilty and make restitution for a concurrent sentence. After I entered my plea the prosecutor wanted to hold sentencing until after my codefendant's trial. I instructed my attorney to inform the judge that Judge Evans was holding my case sub curie pending the disposition of Talbot County. Furthermore, I had made no agreement to testify against my codefendant. The prosecutor told the court that he saw no reason that I couldn't be sentenced today adding that I had also stolen an outboard motor from down the road. I told my attorney to object because I wasn't charged for stealing an outboard motor. I hadn't given a statement. It was irrelevant as to sentencing and the plea of guilty was based upon a concurrent sentence. The judge stood up saying that all of his trouble came from the western side of the bridge and he takes everything into consideration, circumstantial or not, before passing sentence on a man. I looked over my shoulder and one of the guards who escorted me to court from the Maryland House of Corrections held his hand up indicating a sentence of five years. The judge sentenced me to serve three years consecutive to the sixty-four years. On the counselor table there was a metal water pitcher. I grabbed it and hurled it at the judge."

"You threw a water pitcher at a judge?" Mark asked with a huge grin.

"I did. And I paid dearly for it."

"I bet!" Mark laughed aloud.

"I obtained my G.E.D., read Reader's Digest to enhance my vocabulary, and studied law. The eight-year consecutive sentences were run concurrent and the reduced to four years. The three years was reduced to one year giving me a five year sentence. I was sent to camp and assigned to work in Governor Marvin Mandell's mansion. I polished his shoes, curried his Collie, played pool with the State Troopers in their barracks, and ate his steaks. Paroled, I made five trips to Florida in search of my wife and daughters. In 1974 I located my wife's brother living in a trailer in Orlando. Early one morning I left two of my friends asleep at my father's house, drove to the trailer, broke in by picking the lock, and stole my wife's brother's address book. After finding my wife's name I wrote the address and phone number down and returned the book.

"One block from the trailer there was a phone booth in the front of a Seven-Eleven. I stopped, dialed the number and Dayle answered.

'Bill?' She asked, her voice trembling, 'How did you find me?'

Ignoring her question, I asked how the kids were.

'They're fine. I'm married.'

"My daughters didn't know who I was, they thought her husband was their father and called him daddy. It was a short conversation. I was devastated. I had lost everything that I cared about when the game ended, while the police went home to their families. I was much more intelligent now. I knew the law. I could pick locks and turn off alarms. And I had nothing left to lose.

"I returned to my father's house and picked up my friends, Kenny and Buddy Butler. I had recently purchased a new 1974 Datsun pickup truck. I stopped at a Seven-Eleven, bought a case of Budweiser and crawled into the bed of a truck closing the caps door. Kenny drove to Fort Lauderdale. As we were proceeding down Main Street I opened the window to the cap and tossed empty beer cans at the police cruiser behind us. He pulled the truck over and everyone wanted to know what my problem was. I told them that I had found my wife and daughters, they were living in Jacksonville.

Let's go there, that's what we came here for. Kenny argued.

I can't!

Why can't you?' Buddy wanted to know.

How can I walk into two little girls lives who don't know who I am and call another man daddy and tell them that I'm their daddy? I can't do that to them! The cop was sympathetic to us and let us go. I took the remainder of my case of beer, walked to the ocean's edge, and continued drinking. Kenny and Buddy took turns asking what I was going to do. Gazing out over the ocean, watching the waves roll to shore and froth.

"Finally, I said, "If you want popcorn, you go to a popcorn stand. If you want pussy, you go to a whorehouse."

"Where do you go if you want money?"

You're fucking nuts! Kenny and Buddy concluded. Twenty three bank robberies later, the Feds agreed."

"You robbed 23 banks?" Mark asked, grinning.

"Not exactly. The feds circulated a flyer listing 21 known bank robberies credited to the Hooker Gang. There were five named participants. The banks robbed were on the eastern seaboard – from Maine to Florida. I was found guilty of robbing a bank in New Freedom, Pennsylvania and not guilty of robbing a bank in Spruce Pine, North Carolina.

"In Harrisburg, Pennsylvania Judge Nealon sentenced me to serve 15 years under the provision of Title 18 U.S.C. 4205(b)(2) which allowed me to be released at the parole board's discretion. I started out in segregation at Lewisburg, Pennsylvania. That's where I first met Jimmy Burke. In the movie Goodfellas he's called Jimmy Conley. When I was transferred to Atlanta, Georgia Jimmy was there. In 1977 I was transferred to McNeil Island in Washington State. It reminded me of Alcatraz. The only way on or off the island was by ferry. In early April I was working the night shift in the psych ward. The prisoners were locked in their rooms. My job was to make routine rounds to check on them. I had a desk, typewriter, color TV, and a bathtub. The FBI circulated a flyer across the Eastern Seaboard crediting "the Hooker Gang" with 21 known bank robberies. The flyer listed the names of the banks, location, mode of operation, described the manner each bank was robbed, and the amount of money taken from each bank. Twice the FBI tried and failed to indict me for a bank robbery in Bristol, Tennessee. In that robbery $104,000 was taken. In one year, I bought nine new cars, lost $31,000 in Las Vegas at Caesar's Palace in a weekend. I was a high roller! Tom Jones was the featured singer at Caesar's and on closed circuit TV Evel Knievel attempted to jump Snake Canyon.

Anyway, I went from federal penitentiary in Lewisburg to Atlanta to McNeil Island."

"So that's when you were placed in the witness protection program?"

"No! But that's when I met Jerry and Richard and we planned to build Octopool. I also met John Adams in Chicago. He placed a bomb in a federal courthouse and blew up newspaper reporter Don Boyles in Arizona in his car. John made a deal to cooperate for life in protective custody. He regretted his decision because he couldn't imagine spending the rest of his life in that cell.

When I appeared before the parole board, my release was set for 1979. It was then that I learned there were three stages of the program. In custody, out of custody, and out of custody with funding – to be determined at the time of my release.

From the window in my cell I saw a printing company across the street. I wrote a letter to the warden asking permission to write people for assistance. He encouraged it! So I looked the phone number up in the yellow pages and called to get a price for 500 preaddressed enveloped and to have a 2-page letter printed 500 times. I asked if the packages could be through an attorney so they would have to be opened in my presence. No problem. He quoted a price and I called my friend in Maryland Bobby Jenkins and he sent the printer a money order. I prepared a 2-page letter and mailed that to the printer.

One week later three boxes were delivered and opened in my presence. Postage was free for federal prisoners at that time. Myself, Jerry, Richard and John each addressed 25 envelopes sending them to churches, TV and radio stations all over the country. My name, prison number and address were printed on the envelopes. The paper was beige and with a matching envelope.

In a week Jerry was to be released and relocated to Dayton, Ohio. His girlfriend, Lynn Bailey had quit her job and was relocating with him. Jerry promised to write.

Jerry was released and the U.S. Marshals called me out threatening possible criminal charges for the letters mailed off. I showed them the letter sent to the warden and his response.

That's the dirtiest trick I ever saw! the senior U.S. Marshal shouted. You will be released with funding, but any responses from your letters will be returned.' And that's how I got into the witness protection program.

Jerry wrote. He sent his phone number, and he had changed his last name to Burns. When I was released, I was relocated to Cleveland, Ohio and I changed my name to Burns. U.S. Marshall Pete Elliot told me that I was being given a new lease on life. That ended today!"

"Who put the contract on you and why?"

"I never found that out. The night Thomas Colvin was murdered in the prison's theater, he was seated two rows in front of me. The State wasn't able to establish a motive."

Overnight Bill went from earning upwards of twenty thousand dollars a month to less than five thousand. His overhead between the two stores, house, apartment, vehicles, boat and dock rental was more than ten thousand a month.

Beth's parents approved of Bill and so did her son, Danny, who went from being an unruly brat to being the best mannered kid in the neighborhood. Bill soon learned that Dan Ruffing was Beth's ex husband and Danny's father. And Dan had a reputation for causing problems for anyone Beth dated. He had chased George down the street swinging a chain once. But Dan liked and respected Bill, so there were no more problems. More and more, Bill began staying overnight at Beth's parents house. Beth brought a stray dog home and it scratched every door in the house. One by one, Bill took the doors off the hinges, carried them to the garage and refinished them. The house was on creekside, recently rebuilt after being destroyed by a tornado. There was no backyard. From the patio to the creek it was nothing but mounds of dirt. Bill leveled the dirt, planted seed, and topped it with straw. Three months later, they were enjoying the yard. Playing crochet, fishing at the water's edge. George planted a garden next to the house and paid to have a shed built. As time passed, and payments weren't made, Bill's possessions started being repossessed. First, the El Dorado from the house. Lee bought an older customized silver Dodge van with a black stripe. Next, the boat was repossessed. When Bill went to see Mark at his office, he parked on a side street, and the Trans-Am was repossessed. Bill purchased a 1975 silver and maroon Dodge Charger and paid cash.

Beth introduced Bill to Otto John. He lived two blocks from the house. Otto was retired from Jeep, worked in his garage making blowers for engines, drank beer, and kept two kegs on tap. One in his garage, the other in his basement where he boasted the bar never closed. He was quite the character. Thin, average height. He had gray hair with a crown. Once a year, Otto looked forward to his taking a car to the Salt Flats in Nevada. It was through Otto that Bill met Frank "Butch" Hardy. Otto had purchased a home locksmith correspondence course. But, like everything else, he set that on a shelf and let it collect dusk. Butch asked if he could do the lessons, and now Otto's license hung proudly on display above the bar in his basement.

Butch Hardy was six feet, a hundred eighty pounds, with curly brown hair, a mustache, and brown eyes. He was quite the ladies man. There was something in his character that attracted women to him like moths to a flame. He portrayed himself as just a good old country boy. Butch used Otto's license to order locksmith tools and opened a business, Hardy Recovery Service repossessing cars and trucks for banks, loan companies, and used car dealerships. Bill was in need of money, so when Butch asked if he was interested in making some extra cash at night, the only question Bill asked was when did he start.

"You can start tonight." Butch offered.

"How much are you going to pay me, five hundred dollars a night?" Bill joked.

"I hope a flock of bird dogs fly out of my ass if I pay you five hundred dollars a night, Burns!"

During the day, Bill worked at the store. At night he was at Beth's house, Otto John's, Bronco Billy's or out repossessing vehicles.

Butch lived with Bonnie Hardy. They weren't married. Bonnie was his aunt by marriage. She had married Butch's uncle "Snook". Snook had a work related accident and hurt his back requiring hospitalization for several months, and while he was in the hospital Butch started dating Bonnie. What pissed Snook off was Butch maxed out his credit cards forcing him to file bankruptcy. When he was released from the hospital, Bonnie moved in with Butch.

Cindy Meyers lived right around the corner from Beth on Vistamar Drive. Sharon Johnson and her husband "Billy" lived in a small rural house in Sylvania. On Friday night everyone would gather at Bronco Billy's, or, the Rodeo bar. Billy and Sharon both worked at Jeep. Billy's father, Babe Johnson, also worked at Jeep and he owned a farm named, Lazy Acres, on Douglas Road in Temperance, Michigan. Sharon and Beth spent much of their childhood at the farm riding and grooming the horses.

Bill paid a second months rent at the house for Lee and Jenny. When he went to the house to check on them, he found everything gone. There wasn't a piece of furniture, a note nothing. Enraged, he started driving through the neighborhoods, up one road and down another. About a mile away, in the neighborhood of West lake, Bill spotted Lee's van parked in the driveway of a gray ranch house. He parked at the curb, walked to the front door, and knocked. There was no answer.

"Open up, or I'm coming in!" Bill yelled. When the door wasn't answered, he walked to his car, opened the trunk, grabbed a tire iron, and walked to the rear of the house intending to pry open a bedroom window. A police officer stepped to the corner of the house, and asked. "What are you doing?" Before he could explain, Jenny stepped out the back door, and announced. "I called the police, Bill. We didn't know what else to do. We've got to put the kids first!"

"You could have left a note. Have I been unfair with you?"

"Do you want him arrested for trespassing?" The officer asked Jenny.

"No!" Jenny replied. "We just don't want any problems." The officer left, and Jenny invited Bill inside.

"Is this how we do things?" Bill asked Lee. Lee frowned, and apologized.

"The only thing that I care about is the bar that Bonnie bought me. You can have everything else!"

"I'm sorry." Jenny said, hugging Bill's neck. "Your showing up caught us by surprise."

"That's alright. How are the kids?" Bill asked.

"Todd's at school and Missy just started kindergarden. They're doing good. Missy misses you, and asks where her uncle Bill is."

Hearing that, Bill smiled. He and Lee exchanged phone numbers, and Bill returned to Toledo.

\* \* \*

Butch was complaining more and more about his hip hurting and walking with a limp favoring his left leg. Not long afterward, he was diagnosed with cancer and in need of a hip replacement.

After surgery, Butch had to go through Chemo-therapy. After each treatment, he returned home, laid on his couch and puked his guts into a metal bucket. At night, Bonnie would go with Bill to repo cars. There was always a chance of his getting beaten, or shot. Bill took all of the risks, but he didn't mind supporting Butch. They had become more than just friends, they were partners. At least, that was how he felt.

\* \* \*

Bill often thought of the night when he and Beth met Billy and Sharon Johnson at the Rodeo bar. It was his first time meeting Billy. He was big, burly, and sporting a full growth of beard. They were sitting at a table near the band. When the girls left the table to use the powder room. Billy asked. "You do know that Dan is Beth's ex husband?"

On the ride back to Beth's house, Bill asked her. "Is Dan your ex husband?"

She grinned and replied. "Ugh. Yeah! But I didn't think you would hire him if I told you that."

"Are there anymore surprises?"

"Probably!" Beth grinned.

Bill approached Dan at work. "I know that you are Danny's dad and I want you to know that I would never want to come between you and your son."

"It's all good!" Dan grinned.

One night Beth had another surprise. She announced that she was pregnant. Joyce and George were both elated and pushed Bill towards his becoming a part of the family.

When Dan heard the news, he told Bill. "That bitch ain't pregnant!"

One month later, Bill married Beth in a small ceremony at a local church.

A few days later, Bonnie called the house for Bill. The call was short, and awkward. Bill felt terrible. Nothing in his life had ever worked out as he planned.

Beth was addicted to downers, mostly Valium and Qualudes. And, she smoked marijuana routinely. The biggest problem was she wrecked cars faster than Bill could repair them. And her drug use was creating more and more problems. Bill let it be known that if anyone sold her drugs, they would answer to him. Bill backed his words with action and his reputation for being a no nonsense kind of guy quickly spread among the local drug dealers.

* * *

Bill maintained the apartment at Tamaron for Debbie. Every morning she dressed, walked across the street, and opened the store. One day she arrived to find the door padlocked by the IRS and there was a red and yellow sticker on the door. She returned to the apartment and called Bill with the disheartening news. That night the store was burglarized, the entire contents stolen. Debbie reported the theft to the police the next morning. Fortunately for Bill, he had insurance.

For the next three months Bill paid the rent at Tamaron and made sure that Debbie didn't go hungry. She had been loyal, and that meant everything to Bill. Eventually, Debbie moved back to Cleveland to live with her sister.

* * *

Jerry called from Chicago and asked Bill if he would be interested in the video equipment and supplies at the store in Shamburg. They were his for the taking! Jerry just wanted to collect the insurance.

Bill rented a U-HAUL truck, drove it to Chicago, and at midnight he backed-up to the rear door. Jerry unlocked the door and they began emptying the store. There were video recorders, thousands of videos - some still in the plastic wrapper. As they prepared to leave, Bill unscrewed the cylinder lock in the front door, giving the appearance of a burglary.

Bill drove the U-Haul to Bobby Hardin's condo and sold him the entire contents - throwing the popcorn machine in for free.

Then Bill called Lee and stopped by to pick up the bar. Little Missy was anxiously waiting for Bill to get there.

She ran from the house, hugged his neck, and scolded him for his not coming to see her more often.

Once again, Jenny apologized and hugged Bill affectionately. Lee simply grinned, and helped Bill load the bar.

# CHAPTER TWENTY-ONE
# BUCKEYE AUTO AND TRUCK

After closing the Rodeo bar one night, Bill, Beth, and Billy were driving around the suburbs of Sylvania smoking a joint, laughing, and having fun. Suddenly, a drunken Bill stopped the car, ran into someone's backyard, unplugged a bug light, and ran back to the car. About a half mile further down the road a white horse was grazing alongside the road. Billy noticed a halter on the horse and dared Beth to ride the horse to his house, which was less than two miles away. Beth hopped out of the car, approached the horse, rubbed its nose, grabbed the halter and swung herself up onto its back. She rode off at a slow gallop. At Billy's house, Beth and Billy argued over whose horse it was - his, or, hers. Billy argued that he saw the horse first. Beth argued that she rode it to his house. Sharon woke up, and screamed. "Get that fucking horse out of my backyard!" Now, it was Beth's horse. Billy said that he would keep the bug light. Billy thoughtfully suggested that Babe might let Beth board the horse at Lazy Acres.

The following day, Bill drove Beth to see Babe. "Absolutely not!" He said, adding. "But his neighbor, Harry Sweet, might let you board the horse there."

Bill drove Beth to see Harry Sweet. Bill wanted no part of this, so he stayed in the car. Beth returned saying. "He's not interested in boarding the horse, but he might buy it. He's going to follow up to Billy's with his horse trailer." Arriving at Billy and Sharon's house on Sellers Road, Bill quickly went into the house. Harry bought the horse, but he wanted a receipt. A friend of Billy's, Ralph, wrote the receipt and signed the name, Bill Ash.

Two weeks later, the owner of the horse located it at Harry Sweets and called the police. The police followed Harry to Billy's house, and Billy told the authorities that he woke up one morning to find Bill and Beth in his backyard with the horse.

Bill was charged and arranged along with Beth. They were both released on a One thousand dollar personal recognize bond.

A federal parole officer from Toledo, Fritz Snyder, showed up unannounced at the house and informed Bill that he was being returned to active supervision.

"I'm not on federal parole!" Bill argued. "U.S. Marshal Pete Elliott in Cleveland told me that I was on my own two years ago."

"Do you have anything showing that you were released? Otherwise, you were simply on unsupervised parole."

\* \* \*

Bill and Beth drove directly to Billy and Sharon's house. "Why did you tell the police that I stole the horse?" Bill asked, angrily.

"What was I supposed to tell them?" Billy chuckled.

At the preliminary hearing, Billy said the police report was inaccurate, that only Beth was in the backyard with the horse. Instead of dropping the charge against Bill, the female magistrate revoked the personal recognize bonds requiring cash bonds, and remanded Bill and Beth to the Monroe County Jail.

Bond was posted and they were both released, pending trial.

\* \* \*

Bill was driving down Summit Street when a boarded up business caught his eye. He thought that it would be a great location for a video store. Beth's father, George, agreed. George and Bill decided to go into business together, opening POINT PLACE CAMERA AND VIDEO. Together, they rented the building, and spent countless hours remodeling. They gutted the inside, replaced the floor, added a showroom, a rest room, and secured the premises with an alarm. Bill called Chet and commissioned him to make a sign to hang above the building and to letter the windows. Then, Bill borrowed the video rentals from Bobby Hardin. And George used his credit to floor plan video equipment through RCA. Financing was set up. Bill advertised a FREE video camera if you agree to rent 100 weekly rentals from us. Beth's mother Joyce opened and closed the store, the rental business was growing.

* * *

Butch introduced Bill to Cliff Trombly. Cliff owned Buckeye Auto and Truck on LaGrange Street in Toledo. He was short, not well dressed, with messy brown hair and brown eyes. Some of his employees drove tow trucks, while others worked in the salvage yard. Cliff also towed and stored Police impound vehicles. His secretary, Jennie, was short, thin, wore glasses, and had long brown hair that fell to her waist that she normally kept in a ponytail.

Cliff offered to pay Bill three hundred dollars for every 1978-79 Buick Regal, or, Oldsmobile Cutlass that he brought him - no questions asked.

Butch introduced Bill to Ray and Marsha Lindsay. They lived in a modest home on fifteen acres near the airport. Ray raised chickens, pigs, and a Peacock ran freely on his property. Ray was tall, thin, with brown hair and brown eyes. Marsha was average size with dirty blonde hair. Since he married her, Ray had turned his life around. She was quiet, shy, and worked as a clerk in a local store. Ray lived to hunt, and fish. When he did work, he was an electrician.

Butch also introduced Bill to Jim Pack, a retired Toledo police officer who now lived in Tennessee.

For Thanksgiving, a feast was planned at Ray and Marsha's house. Ray planned to roast a pig. A black family down the street offered to roast the pig for twenty dollars, but Ray took pride in wanting to do it himself.

After digging a pit and making a spit that turned, Ray chose a pig and shot it squarely in the head with a twenty-two rifle. He tossed the pig into the back of his pick-up and before reaching his house, the pig came back to life. Ray stopped the truck, grabbed a hammer, and began beating it in the head. Then, he hung it from a tree and gutted it. "I'll get Marsha up at five o'clock tomorrow morning. With her help, I'll get the pig on the spit and start the fire."

The next morning, it rained. Using two sheets of plywood Ray made a lean-to to shelter the fire and the pig from the rain. By ten o'clock when the pig turning on the spit reached the top, it flopped over. Ray tried tying the pig to the spit with wire - to no avail. The pig wasn't cooked at noon, or, two o 'clock, or, four o'clock. At five, Ray kicked the pig into the spit and sent Marsha to Kentucky Fried Chicken to buy two buckets of chicken.

* * *

Butch lived at 902 Bassett Street, a dead end street in Toledo. It was a small one bedroom, one bath, house with a concrete roofed porch. Two blocks away, he rented a large garage that most people didn't ever see. It was in a totally inconspicuous area. One of Cliff's employees. Rick Fritz, helped Butch work on vehicles in his spare time. Rick stood six feet, was thin, with short brown hair and hazel eyes. He was much younger than Butch, but having worked in a salvage yard he had learned a lot about cars.

Cliff rented two buildings. One directly behind Buckeye Auto and Truck, the other behind the Dark Horse restaurant on Telegraph Road. Cliff could literally drive a vehicle into his salvage yard, open a gate at the rear, and drive it into the rented garage. Rather than pay Bill and Butch in cash, Cliff offered vin tags and titles from vehicles in the salvage yard.

Otto John had factory rivets that he had stolen when he worked at Jeep. The star rivets are used by General Motors, Chrysler, and nearly all new car factories when attaching vin tags to the dashboard.

Ray Lindsay told Bill about an auction that was in a barn in Grayson, Kentucky. It was a cash auction unlike anything Ray had ever seen before. The following Thursday, Bill went to the auction with Ray. The vehicles were run through a barn, auctioned off, and the owner paid in cash.

Cliff gave Bill a title to a 1979 Ford four-wheel drive F-150. Butch switched the vin tag, removed the metal serial identification numbers from beneath and behind the seat, welded and restamped the numbers on the frame of the truck, and replaced the locks. The next week Bill sold the truck at Grayson Auto Auction. The owner, Ralph, listed the vehicle sold by Burns Auto Sales. Butch assured Bill that the truck would pass any inspection!

At an auction on Telegraph Road, Bill bought a 1981 white Monte Carlo for fifteen hundred dollars. The car had a salvage title, having been stolen and recovered. The odometer displayed 15,000 actual miles. But there was no front end, doors, trunk, or tires. It was a shell with an engine and transmission.

Cliff wanted Bill to steal a flat bed truck from a county fifty miles away. Bill offered him a deal. He would steal the truck. Then he would steal a Monte Carlo identical to the one he had purchased and he wanted Cliff to switch the body to his frame. Cliff agreed. The Monte Carlo had red velour interior, air-conditioning, cruise control, power windows, doors, and locks. After switching the vin tag, Bill made an appointment to have the vehicle inspected by the Ohio State Police. It passed without a problem, and a clear title was issued.

* * *

Once a month Beth received a monthly welfare check and food stamps. She sold the food stamps to Butch. One month, Butch paid her in advance. Then, when she got the food stamps she sold them to someone else. Butch was livid. He told her. "You'll never get over on me again, big girl!"

Beth grinned, and replied. "Oh yes, I will!" Bill finally had enough of Beth's bullshit. He moved out, renting a two bedroom apartment in Perrysburg at Perrysburg Village. It was directly across from the Holiday Inn and the French Quarters. Terry Trezinski and his girlfriend, Jackie, rented the second bedroom. Terry sold drugs and hustled pool. Mostly, he simply enjoyed life. Every day was a holiday and every meal a feast.

* * *

Ray Lindsay told Bill about a house around the corner on Dorr Street. It had been vacant for more than two years. Bill called the number on the sign and the owner agreed to meet him at the house. It was one bedroom ranch home that sat on fifteen acres, and the yard was filled with rotting wooden pallets. It was in dire need of repairs, but Bill had a vision. He purchased the house on a Land contract for $38,000.

George and Joyce told Bill that Beth just needed her own place, that if he were to take her back she would be fine. So, Bill did. He loved the family!

At night, there were bonfires at the house where Bill burned trash and pallets as he cleaned up the yard. Bonnie Hardy had two daughters, Cindy and Cheryl. Cheryl lived in Tennessee. Cindy was married. She, her husband Carl, along with their two daughters lived in Bonnie and Snook's house on South Otter Creek Road in LaSalle, Michigan. Carl's father owned Carter Construction and Carl worked as a carpenter. Bill hired Carl and his father to remodel the house, gutting the inside.

Cliff gave Bill a second title for a 1979 Ford four-wheel drive truck. Rick Fritz stole a Ford truck from an apartment complex off of Secor Road. Behind Bill's house on Dorr Street, Rick jacked the cab up, welded and restamped the frame, and switched the vin tag. Then, in Butch's garage, he painted the truck black. Billy Johnson bought the truck.

* * *

Rick and Butch bought a title for a 1977 Ford F-150 four-wheel drive pick-up. Rick stole a 1979 Ford F-150 four-wheel drive, switched the vin plate, welded the frame, and restamped it. Then Butch asked Bill to take Rick to the auction in Grayson when he went.

Cliff gave Bill a title to a 1977 CJ-7 four-wheel drive Jeep. Bill stole a brand new Jeep off the lot of a new car dealership. The Jeep was a metallic brown CJ-7 with a hardtop and a new Meyer's snow plow. There was no place for the vin tag on the newer model, so part of the dash from the 1977 model was used. It looked like it came from the factory! Bill paid an associate of Butch's to weld the frame and restamp the serial number. Jim Pack offered $5,000. for the Jeep - upon delivery.

* * *

In Monroe, Beth entered a guilty plea for Theft. And, the charges against Bill for the stolen horse were dismissed. Beth's attorney assured her that she would be given probation, at sentencing.

* * *

Ralph Justice owned the auto auction in Grayson, Kentucky. He was a big man, in his late forties - and he was truly one of the good old boy's. Straight forward, no nonsense. If he had something to say, he got right to the point. Rick drove his and Butch's truck to the auction. Bill drove the Jeep and Beth followed in Bill's white Monte Carlo. After the auction, Bill's plan was to deliver the Jeep to Jim Pack in Tennessee.

When Rick's truck ran through the auction, a local farmer bought it. Ten minutes later, Ralph told Bill. "We've got a problem. The numbers on the truck match, but the suspension changed in 1979. The 1976 through 1978 were different. The guy still wants the truck, but he wants a receipt along with it."

Bill told Rick, and he agreed to write the receipt. From that day forward, to protect himself, vehicles with an Ohio title were registered to Burns Auto Sales.

Bill and Beth rode in the Monte Carlo. Rick drove the Jeep and followed them to Tennessee. After dropping the Jeep off to Jim Pack, and being paid upon delivery - the trio returned to Toledo.

One good turn deserves another. Rick Fritz needed a Chevrolet four wheel drive truck. Bill and Beth drove him to Cleveland. When they found a nice truck in an apartment complex, they dropped Rick off. It was after three o' clock in the morning. Rick walked up the driver's side of the truck, pried the wing vent open, reached inside and unlocked the door. In less than a minute, he started the engine, backed up, and drove out of the parking lot. The trucks engine died, and Bill circled back. As Rick got into the car, a car fell in behind them. Bill stopped at the corner, then turned left. The car followed closely behind. As a police cruiser approached from the opposite direction the car behind Bill began flashing its lights. As he stopped to talk to the officer, Bill took a quick right, and dropped Rick off. After two more turns, Bill stopped to hide his tools beneath some bushes. Then, he continued down the road. At the expressway, Bill turned around to go back and pick Rick up. Cruisers came from every direction blocking the car in. When questioned, Bill admitted that he picked a guy up and gave him a ride to the expressway. A search of the car produced a broken ignition. Bill explained that he worked as a recovery agent for Hardy Recovery Service in Toledo.

Bill and Beth were charged in Cleveland for Attempted Auto Theft and Burglary Tools. Bond was placed the next day and they were released. Bill picked up his tools and they returned to Toledo. Rick Fritz hitch-hiked back to Toledo.

## CHAPTER TWENTY-TWO
## BINGO!

When Bill purchased the house on Dorr Street, he gave the owner twenty-five hundred dollars in cash and agreed to payments of six hundred dollars a month for sixty months. In five years, the house would be paid for! But his vision was to insure the house and contents for sixty thousand dollars. In a year or two, the house would be destroyed by fire. He would collect the insurance, pay off the mortgage, and build a new house further back from the road.

In need of money, Bill placed an ad in the Toledo Blade to sell his Monte Carlo for fifty-five hundred dollars. Sergeant Schroder of the Toledo Police Department and his brother, an attorney, bought the car.

Cliff's secretary, Jennie, kept two sets of books. In one set when she paid for a stolen vehicle, she wrote. "Psycho Auto Parts." Cliff was buying more and more vehicles with salvage titles. It was a lucrative business, switching the body and vin tag, then making an appointment to send the vehicle to the Ohio State Police to be inspected. The salvage title was then reissued to a clear Ohio title. The 1978-79 Buick Regal and Oldsmobile Cutlass had full frames, and the car body was easily switched.

Rich McQuire also worked for Cliff at Buckeye Auto and Truck, he worked as the manager and was usually in the office selling used parts. Rich was five feet ten, average weight, with well groomed blonde hair and blue eyes. He was well mannered and his professionalism made him stand apart from the other employees.

\* \* \*

Once a week, Bill made the trip to Grayson, Kentucky. One of the bidders introduced himself to Bill as the Mayor of Portsmith, Ohio. He owned a small car lot and was interested in purchasing vehicles before Bill brought them to the auction. The man was short, well rounded, and slightly balding. He spoke with a Southern drawl and had a pocket full of cash. He offered to meet Bill halfway, or, make the trip to Toledo himself to purchase vehicles. He handed Bill his business card, and said. "Call me, first!"

* * *

If Cliff spotted a vehicle in a parking lot with a dealer tag attached by a magnet, or spring - he stole it. He said the police couldn't check dealer tags on a routine stop. The salvage yard was always busy, the smell of grease, dirt, and burning metal filled the air. Engine and transmission blocks were stacked four feet high. Radiators went into another pile. Vehicles were stacked one on top of another. Once they were stripped of parts, they were crushed and sold for weight. A car crusher came to the salvage yard once a month.

Cliff was given a newer car to part out. The owner was going to report it stolen in three days and collect on the insurance. For Cliff, it was free money! One week later, Cliff was still driving the car. He put a stolen dealer tag on the trunk of the car and drove it to school to pick up his young son. After leaving the school, he was caught on radar doing forty-five in a twenty-five mile an hour zone. Realizing that the car had been reported stolen and he had some drugs in his pocket, he attempted to elude the police. When that failed, he gave his son the drugs and told him to get out of the car and run when he stopped. Cliff was arrested for possession of a stolen vehicle, fleeing and eluding. Bill went to the Toledo jail and posted his bond.

Through their sources, it was known two weeks in advance the police were going to raid Buckeye Auto and Truck. Cliff swore the salvage yard was clean.

Early one morning, when Cliff opened the gates to the salvage yard, the police rushed in. Bill drove over to Butch's house, hooked up a police scanner, and listened to the reports.

At five o 'clock, the police were tired and exasperated. As they prepared to call it quits, on a whim, a young rookie jotted down serial numbers from engines laying in a pile and called those in to the dispatcher.

"Bingo!" The dispatcher excitedly yelled. The vehicle was licensed. He gave the year of the vehicle, the make, model, name of the current owner - and the current address.

Eight times the dispatcher yelled "Bingo!" following the same process. And each time, sitting at the kitchen table sipping a cup of coffee, Bill took notes writing the information on a piece of paper.

The following morning the Toledo police were flooded with reports of stolen vehicles. The detectives were sure there was a leak of information within the department. Every vehicle the dispatcher had announced had been reported stolen and vanished overnight. Was it a massive conspiracy, they wondered.

Cliff and Jennie were arrested on multiple charges, the gates to the salvage yard locked.

One week later, Cliff and Jeanie were released on bond, and the salvage yard was allowed to reopen. The padlock remained on the police impound lot, and Cliff was not permitted to tow vehicles for the City of Toledo until further notice.

\* \* \*

Jerry came from Chicago, desperate to make some money. Bill told Jerry about the police raiding Buckeye Auto and Truck, the dispatcher yelling "Bingo!" and everything that followed. Jerry laughed so hard, it hurt.

Five blank titles were stolen from the Licensing Bureau on Sylvania Avenue. For One Hundred dollars each, Bill bought three. He stole two vehicles from long term parking at the Toledo Express Airport. Butch made a set of keys for each car, and then Bill simply typed the name, address, make, model, year of the vehicle, and serial number on each title.

Jerry's story was that he was going through a divorce, needed some quick cash, so he was selling the car that he had bought for his wife. He successfully sold one of the vehicles for cash to a used car dealership. At the corner of Dorr and Alexis Road he drove into the lot of Cars-R-Us, not knowing the owner was a Toledo police officer. When he ran the vin number, the name of the owner wasn't the same as the name on the title. Sensing that something was wrong, Jerry walked from the car lot, crossed the street, and was apprehended by the police between two apartment buildings. Released on bail, Jerry told Bill and Butch the Toledo detectives were looking for a woman who was using credit cards that came from a purse she left beneath the seat of her stolen car.

Bill recalled Bonnie going shopping the day before. Returning, she commented about some guy trying to get her license plate number, and she had since dyed her hair black. Troubling to Bill was that his partner, Butch, had never mentioned finding a purse.

"I was also questioned about a salvage yard. Apparently, there's an active investigation."

Bill knew that Jerry had cooperated, he simply knew too much information. What Jerry knew that was of value to the detectives was the police scanner, the dispatcher yelling "Bingo!" and how the cars came up disappearing. The one thing that Jerry did not know was where the cars went.

* * *

Rick Fritz was arrested, and released on bond. Shortly after his release, Billy Johnson received a call requesting that he take his black Ford truck to the State Police Inspection Station in Walbridge, Ohio.

Billy complied. And, the truck passed inspection.

One week later, Billy Johnson was asked to return with the truck. The previous owner identified the truck by a make-shift strap holding the gas tank in place.

Simultaneously the Toledo police raided Cliff and Butch Hardy's chop shops. Inside the building behind the Dark Horse restaurant on Telegraph Road were rear clips of vehicles stacked from the floor to the ceiling. From Butch's garage the police recovered three stolen vehicles.

In Tennessee, the authorities seized Jim Pack's Jeep.

Arrest warrants were issued for Bill, and Beth. For some reason, the police thought that Burns Auto Sales belonged to "Beth Burns". She was arrested at her parents house for warrants issued out of Portsmouth, Ohio.

Butch was released on a One thousand dollar personal recognize bond.

George retained an attorney in Portsmith, Ohio and posted Beth's bond.

Bill eluded the police. He obtained an Ohio State Identification card under the alias of Benny Louis Hamilton and a Maryland Driver's license under the alias of James Lee Roberts. He was later arrested in Pirelli Park, Michigan in a campground in a 1984 37' Ex Caliber Motor Home stolen from Medina, Ohio. It cost $38,000. In the rear of the Motor Home there was a Queen size bed and a bath consisting of a shower, toilet, and sink. It was equipped with a stove and microwave, refrigerator, two color televisions, and a stereo system. It had chrome wheels, a dual rear axle, and two roof air-conditioners. Bill used his third stolen blank title for the Motor Home. Also, in Bill's possession was a stolen 1976 Camaro, metallic silver with a black racing stripe. The vehicle had been stolen in Maryland and the vin tag switched.

Every night there was a party at the campground. Bill tapped a keg of beer and cooked on the grill. If you were a friend, you were invited. No one ever left early. Sometimes the party continued until daylight.

When Beth was released on bond. she went to see Bill at the campground. In three days, he planned to purchase a temporary tag for the ExCaliber and drive it to Mexico.

At midnight, Bill drove to the public restroom. There were toilets, showers, urinals, and sinks to accommodate the campers needs. As Bill washed his hands, a man walked inside the block building, used the urinal, then stood next to him washing his hands. In the mirror, Bill saw the man's hair was slightly ruffled, like it was purposely done. He was wearing a white shirt with the sleeves partially rolled up, and cuffed. Dark dress pants, and black laced shoes - the kind that cop's wear! Bill never once spoke on it, but his gut feeling was that he had just been I.D.'d.

The following morning there was a loud pounding on the door of the Motor Home. Bill pulled the curtain back and looked out. There were U.S. Marshals, State Troopers, the Monroe County Sheriff's Department, and

Federal Agents surrounding the Motor Home.

"Come out with your hands up!"

* * *

Beth was serving a year's probation for the Theft charge in Monroe. Her probation was revoked.

The feds took Bill to the federal prison in Milan, Michigan and held him in segregation pending a revocation hearing. He was charged in Monroe for possession of the stolen Motor Home and the stolen Camaro.

Milan claimed that Bill didn't meet the criteria for their population, so Bill filed a Writ of Habeas Corpus in Ann Arbor alleging Cruel and Unusual Punishment. After a hearing lasting four hours a sympathetic judge chastised the treatment, but ruled there was a strong policy in the non-intervention in the overall operation of the federal Bureau of Prison.

After six months in segregation, Bill appeared before the United States Parole Commission for a revocation hearing. Without a new conviction, he was sentenced to serve 42-months.

### Bill Burns

Monroe, Michigan. Bill pled guilty to temporary use of a stolen motor vehicle for a concurrent sentence to his federal sentence with a stipulation valuing the Motor Home under $10,000 and stating that it was returned to the owner within 72 hours.

Cleveland, Ohio. Bill pled guilty. He was sentenced to One-year current to his federal sentence.

Grayson, Kentucky. to avoid a federal investigation involving other people, Bill pled guilty to seventeen counts of receiving and concealing stolen property. He received a concurrent sentence to his federal sentence.

When Bill appeared before the Parole Board. On review, his guidelines were reduced to 24-30 months due to the stipulations in Monroe.

### Beth Burns

Monroe, Michigan. Sentenced to serve One-year for probation violation.
Cleveland, Ohio. Pled guilty. Sentenced to serve One-year at the
women's reformatory in Marysville, Ohio.
Portsmith, Ohio - charges dismissed.
Grayson, Kentucky - charges dismissed.

### Cliff Trombly
Toledo, Ohio. Sentenced to serve 15-years.

### Jeannie
Toledo, Ohio. Sentenced to serve 5 1 /2 years.

### Rick Fritz
Toledo, Ohio. Sentenced to serve 4 1 /2 years.

### Butch Hardy
After a 3-day trial by jury, he was found guilty.
Sentenced to serve One year.

### Jerry Burns
No charges filed.

## ABOUT THE AUTHOR

William Daniel Burns was born in Lakeland, Florida. His family, and those who knew him in his early years called him "Danny." At an early age, he discovered his gift for conning people to get whatever he wanted. At the age of five, he convinced his best friend that two rusty nails and a piece of wood were from George 'Washington's rocking chair and they would someday be worth a whole lot more then his old shiny silver dollar.

When he was seven, his father moved the family to Baltimore, MD. It was a much tougher neighborhood. Danny learned to fight, and hustle. His parents divorced when he was twelve. His younger sister and older brother chose to stay with his mother. Danny chose to live with his father. They returned to live in Florida, and Danny changed his name to "Bill." His father remarried when he was thirteen. Bill quit school, and left home when he was fifteen. He married, and had two beautiful daughters by the age of seventeen - Tina Marie, and Kerri Ann. He was ill-prepared to handle the responsibility, and moved back to the mean streets of Baltimore, where he turned to crime as a means to support his family. The police made a game of that by telling him they rode around in marked cars and wore uniforms, then asked what does a criminal look like. Bill purchased a yellow panel truck and wrote THIEF WAGON across the back and sides in big black bold letters. The game ended with Bill being sent to prison.

Released from prison, he found his wife remarried and his daughters calling another man "daddy." Bill felt that he had nothing left to lose and devoted his life to crime!

Bill returned to federal prison twice. He furthered his education by obtaining his G.E.D., a degree in Commercial Art, and he has the equivalent of a two-year college Associates Degree. Bill has owned a number of successful businesses.

# ABOUT THE AUTHOR

William Daniel Burns was born in Lakeland, Florida. His family, and those who knew him in his early years called him "Danny." At an early age, he discovered his gift for conning people to get whatever he wanted. At the age of five, he convinced his best friend that two rusty nails and a piece of wood were from George 'Washington's rocking chair and they would someday be worth a whole lot more then his old shiny silver dollar.

When he was seven, his father moved the family to Baltimore, MD. It was a much tougher neighborhood. Danny learned to fight, and hustle. His parents divorced when he was twelve. His younger sister and older brother chose to stay with his mother. Danny chose to live with his father. They returned to live in Florida, and Danny changed his name to "Bill." His father remarried when he was thirteen. Bill quit school, and left home when he was fifteen. He married, and had two beautiful daughters by the age of seventeen - Tina Marie, and Kerri Ann. He was ill-prepared to handle the responsibility, and moved back to the mean streets of Baltimore, where he turned to crime as a means to support his family. The police made a game of that by telling him they rode around in marked cars and wore uniforms, then asked what does a criminal look like. Bill purchased a yellow panel truck and wrote THIEF WAGON across the back and sides in big black bold letters. The game ended with Bill being sent to prison.

Released from prison, he found his wife remarried and his daughters calling another man "daddy." Bill felt that he had nothing left to lose and devoted his life to crime!

Bill returned to federal prison twice. He furthered his education by obtaining his G.E.D., a degree in Commercial Art, and he has the equivalent of a two-year college Associates Degree. Bill has owned a number of successful businesses.

In 1988, Bill worked as an independent contractor for O's Auto Sales in Walbridge, Ohio. In 1991, while the owner vacationed in Florida, Bill was left in charge of the business. Several other guys also used the license, but they weren't registered to buy or sell vehicles at the auctions.

On May 28, 1991 Bill left with his girlfriend on a Florida vacation, returning June 8, 1991. A fire occurred at Adrian Auto Auction May 31, 1991, and a murder occurred in Northwood, OH on June 7, 1991. When questioned in regard to the murder, Bill accounted for his whereabouts for the entire vacation.

In 1993 Bill was charged with stolen vehicles in Monroe and Adrian, Michigan.

On the advice of two attorneys Bill pled guilty. At sentencing, he told the judge there was nothing anyone could do when they are signed, sealed, and delivered. That just because he signed the titles, it did not necessarily mean the vehicles were his!

Bill served his sentence, and in 1998, he was transferred to the halfway House in Monroe, Michigan. Ten days before his release, he was charged for the arson of Adrian Auto Auction. The prosecutor contended that his motive for the arson was to destroy incriminating evidence, the titles to the stolen vehicles. Bill filed three formal motions for discovery - none were complied with! He refused plea offers of 10 years, 5 years, and 2 years with credit for six months served. Bill was convicted, and sentenced to serve LIFE. He still maintains his innocence.

Bill is a strong supporter of prison reform. He wants to let the youth of today know that crime, drugs, and violence is not a "game." Bill thanks God for his love, insight, and guidance as he journeys through life. For more information on him, please contact him via www.jpay.com. He is inmate number #189577.

Bonnie selling the pink stuff

Bonnie buried in work at California

Bill at the Sportsman's Show in 1980

Bill, Ralph and Jerry at the apartment in Dayton.

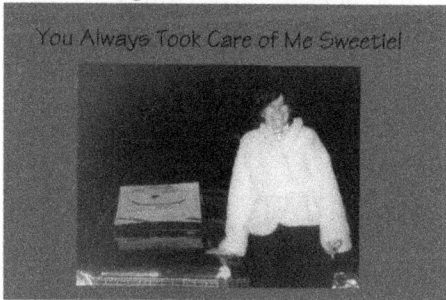

You Always Took Care of Me Sweetie!

Happy Valentines

Happiness comes with little girls' smiles

Bonnie with her gymnastic team at Brecksville High School

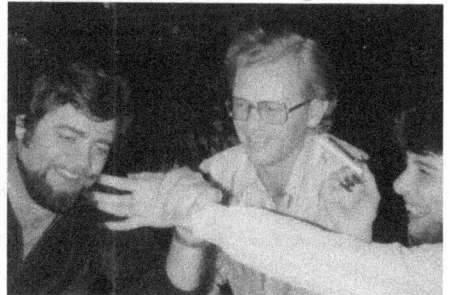

Richard on the right, my biggest disappointment

Bill having fun at bonnie's House

Bobby Hardin was the perfect party helper

Bill and Bonnie. It was love at first sight

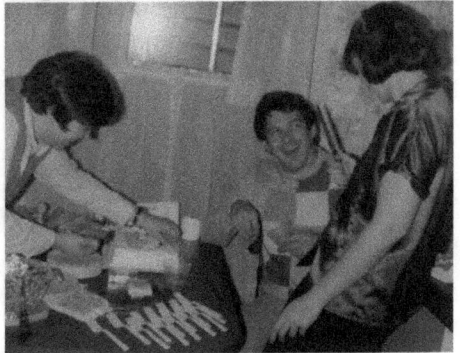

Dottie helping save Bill's cake

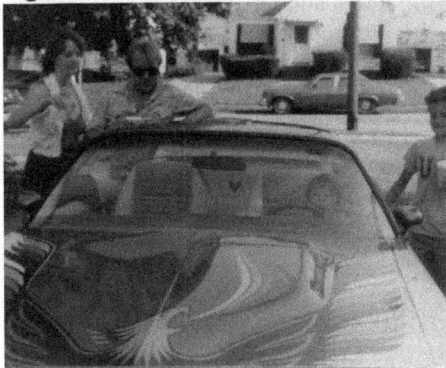

Mark Knevel at Beer Ball Game

Bill with his two favorite things

Jenny and Lee out for a family dinner

Christmas in Chicago. Bill and Bonnie playing Backgammon

Bill & Bonnie in 1980.

Bonnie Sitting in her Valentine's Day present in 1981.

Bill & Bonnie in her house on Ralph Street in 1981.

Bill at his desk at B&H Camera in Toledo, OH in 1984.

Bobby & Mary in Florida in 1986.

Bobby & Mary 1975.

From Left: Karen, Billy, Mary, Sandy in 1975.

Bobby with his daughter, Dusty Dawn.

Mary in front of their home at 587
Riverside Drive in 1979.

Mary 1975.

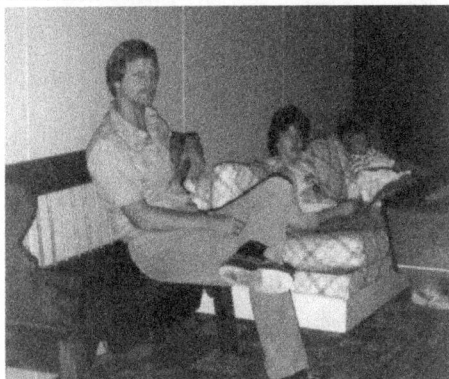

Gorden.

Billy Jenkins, September 1977 (Age 15)

Bill, Jean Staubs & friend 1973

14. Bill with his mother at her trailer in
New Port Ritchie, FL 1974.

Bill in federal prison 1978.

Bill & Jenny. On May 31, 1988 upon
being released from federal prison, Lee
Chambers co-signed for Bill to buy the
Chevrolet IRoc Z-28.

# ORDER MORE EXCITING NOVELS FROM W.D. BURNS!

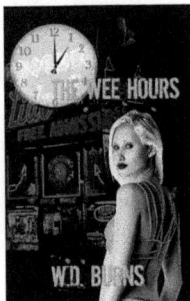

## THE WEE HOURS

Nothing could have prepared Nicole Redman for the brutal murder of her six-year old daughter. Through a cloud of shock and pain, she seeks her daughter's murderer in a world filled with sleazy strip clubs, after-hour joints, and a notorious outlaw biker gang.

She is quickly drawn into a life of illicit sex, drugs, and onto the path of a sadistic hitman.

## PEACHES: WEE HOURS II

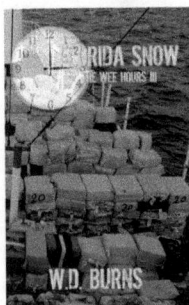

Nicole Redman found herself lost in an unforgiving world of outlaws whom she had grown to love, respect, and understand. Morally bankrupt by the rules of society, the outlaw bikers lived by one rule - an eye for an eye. The brotherhood ran deep, and Nicole 'Peaches' Redman was proud to call the Argots her family. In her wildest dreams, she had never imagined herself becoming a prostitute, a dancer, a biker chick, a murderer, or a reputed drug dealer. When life handed her lemons, she made lemonade.

## FLORIDA SNOW: WEE HOURS III

Hoping to escape a trail of blood and death, Peaches arrives in Florida only to discover that the death toll had just begun. The Argots and the Heathens suddenly find themselves pitted against one another in a vicious drug war, forcing Peaches to fight to save her beloved club. Now, in order to survive she must tame a powerful Columbian Druglord, and outfox an F.B.I. and D.E.A. Task Force.

## SOME KIND OF CROOK

Baltimore, Maryland, 1974. Special Agent H. Thomas Moore of the Towson Office pursued a group of five men who committed 23 known bank robberies across the Eastern Seabord from Maine to Florida. This story is based on the life of the alleged leader.

# ORDER THE ENTIRE
# MEGA HOUSE PUBLICATIONS LINEUP!

## Mega House Publications

Mail: Megahouse Publications
PO Box 122
Brunswick, OH 44212

Name: _____

Address:_____

City/State:_____

Zip:_____

| Quantity | Titles | Price | Total |
|---|---|---|---|
| _____ | The Wee Hours | $12.95 | _____ |
| _____ | The Wee Hours II: Peaches | $12.95 | _____ |
| _____ | The Wee Hours III: Florida Snow | $12.95 | _____ |
| _____ | Some Kind of Crook | $12.95 | _____ |
| _____ | Some Kind of Crook II: Octopool | $12.95 | _____ |
| _____ | Some Kind of Crook III: Framed | $12.95 | _____ |

Add $3.95 for shipping and handling (Via Priority Mail) for
1 book, $5.95 for 2 books , $8.95 for 3-4 books, add $1.95
for each additional book.

Total: $_____
FORMS OF ACCEPTED PAYMENT: Certified or government
 issued checks and Money Order, all mail in order takes 7-10
Business Days to be delivered.
Or, just order online at http://www.megahousepublications.com!

... Megahouse Publica ...
... Box ...
... ock, OR ...

Name _____

Address _____

City/State _____

| Quantity | Title | Price |
|----------|-------|-------|
| | The ... Manual ... | $12.95 |
| | The Workbook Reader | $15.95 |
| | The ... Floor to Front Store ... | $15.95 |
| | Some Kind of ... | $14.95 |
| | Some Kind of ... if a Group | $12.95 |
| | Some Kind of ... not the Father | $9.95 |

Add $2.95 for shipping each online. We'll ship ... for ...
... book ... or ...
... each additional book.

Total _____

TERMS OF ACCEPTABLE PAYMENT: Certified or government
issued checks and Money Order, all mail in order takes ...10
Business Days to be delivered.

... or ... information at http://www.megahouse-publications.com

www.ingramcontent.com/pod-product-compliance
Lightning Source LLC
Chambersburg PA
CBHW060834110426
R18122100001BA/R181221PG42736CBX00027BA/27

9 780996 265164